DAVID MILLER

An Envelope
/
There and Here

SPUYTEN DUYVIL
New York   Paris

Library of Congress Cataloging-in-Publication Data

Names: Miller, David, 1950- author.
Title: An envelope : there and here / David Miller.
Description: New York : Spuyten Duyvil, [2022]
Identifiers: LCCN 2022043705 | ISBN 9781956005967 (paperback)
Subjects: LCGFT: Novels.
Classification: LCC PR9619.3.M47 E58 2022 | DDC 823/.914--dc23/
eng/20220912
LC record available at https://lccn.loc.gov/2022043705

Even though David Miller's stories are full of conscious, indeed self-conscious choices, the writer himself is completely unselfconscious, at least to the extent that he doesn't give a brass monkey what the enemy thinks. He is being himself. His discourse is natural to him, musician and writer. His tone of voice is cool; the unexpected turns in the plot, the apparently false then righted moves, are redolent of improvisations familiar from free jazz.

Anthony Rudolf

I love the constant inconsistency of the book—its author keeps it going, meandering, moving forward and ... its final outcome does not even come as a surprise to us, as it tends to be an entirely different, consistent piece of writing, different from the previous pages of *An Envelope*. In the end of the book the reader finds almost fifty pages meticulously written on the life and times of Gérard de Nerval, the French Romantic, mystical poet who changed the spirit of French letters as he believed in Dream and not Cartesian logic. He believed in Life as well and also in the capacity to preserve the living memory of Life beyond Death, beyond the disappearing and the vanishing. As a French historian indicated once "no one better than Nerval could break those impenetrable doors made of ivory which lead us to the realm of the imaginary." In his last piece but one, somewhat like his master Nerval, David Miller has reached and penetrated indeed those perfect and persistent invisible doors.

Nina Zivancevic

The poet David Miller has worked across genres throughout his career, with writings that challenge conventional boundaries between poetry, short story, life writing and essay. This tendency remains apparent in many of his recent publications: the "children's stories for adults" in *Towards a Menagerie* (Tucson: Chax Press, 2019), which engage with historical writers and artists encountered by the tales' animal heroes; the collaging of autobiographical fragments and theological reflection in his magnificent prose poem sequence *Spiritual Letters* (London: Contraband, 2017 / NY: Spuyten Duyvil, 2022); and, as editor, *The Alchemist's Mind* (Hastings: Reality

Street, 2012), his anthology of narrative prose by poets. The UK poetry scene has, in recent years, become increasingly interested in interdisciplinary, genre-crossing modes such as "creative criticism." (...) David Miller has pioneered such practices in a series of writings dating back to the 1970s. (...) Each genre recognises its double, its othered self, in the moment of cross-genre encounter. Poetry manifests in the wordless strokes of a painting; art history is reflected in the pages of children's fiction; autobiography is sublated in the service of literary criticism, yet becomes truer as autobiography by virtue of having humbled itself. On each occasion, one genre looks into its own eyes when it meets another, becoming more interesting and greater in its own terms through giving itself over to what once seemed external to it.

Matt Martin

Also by David Miller:

The Caryatids, 1975

South London Mix, 1975

Malcolm Lowry and the Voyage that Never Ends, 1976

W.H. Hudson and the Elusive Paradise, 1990

Pictures of Mercy: Selected Poems, 1991

Stromata, 1995

Art and Disclosure: Seven Essays, 1998

The Waters of Marah, 2005

The Dorothy and Benno Stories, 2005

British Poetry Magazines 1914-2000 (with Richard Price), 2006

In the Shop of Nothing: New and Selected Poems, 2007

Black, Grey and White: A Book of Visual Sonnets, 2011

Reassembling Still: Collected Poems, 2014

Matrix I & II, 2020

Some Other Days and Nights, 2021

Afterword, 2022

Circle Square Triangle, 2022

Some Other Shadows, 2022

An Envelope for Silence, 2022

Edited by:

A Curious Architecture: contemporary prose poems (with Rupert Loydell), 1996

The ABCs of Robert Lax (with Nicholas Zurbrugg),1999

Music while drowning: German Expressionist Poems (with Stephen Watts), 2003

The Lariat and other writings by Jaime de Angulo, 2009

The Alchemist's Mind: a book of narrative prose by poets, 2012

In memory of Dodo, with love

Contents

THE DOROTHY AND BENNO STORIES: *CLOTHED WITH A CLOUD*

1.

The discrete: contiguity re-forms the splintered elements, wind-ruffled water's surface, roads spreading out before us in autumnal colours. Something hovers unseen over us and tempts us to brooding presentiments.

Coming up the road from where she'd left her car, Dorothy was troubled—even before entering the old house.

A door, simply enough, opened upon a room with a corpse on the floor; as if she had already known it would be like this. She advanced into the room, and cried out to the figure she saw standing at the opposite end of the space. He vanished through another door, and try as hard as she did to find him, he would not materialise again.

And the face of the dead man. The long, heavy eyelids, and the start of a smile at the mouth. What would he have been able to tell her?

•

Before telephoning for the police, Dorothy had made a search of the house, constructing a map of its design with notations of any details that seemed at all significant in the light of what she'd already discovered. One thing that particularly impressed her was a copy of Frederick van der Meer's *Apocalypse*; it had been left open, and a shaky hand had underlined the following passage:

> Neither bleating nor complaint can be imagined with the Lamb, only silence. His counterfeit, the Beast, has ten horns stupidly distributed on its seven heads; it has no seven eyes, however, and sees but little.
>
> Roaring, flattering, insinuating, it works magic, hypnotises crowds and organises a diabolical cult.

She decided to remove the book to her car; then, having come back into the house, she phoned the local police station.

•

My worry, *my* puzzlement and horror, animated the space where the corpse lay. His lifelessness created a void at the heart of that space; and that void was the source of what I did and said and felt, to cover it over, and resolve the slackness of the ungainly slumped figure and the smile at the mouth which seemed to give a light to the heavy eyelids and the forehead. That stillness, that nothingness: I had to examine and examine again everything I could think of in connection with his death, in order to quell the silence which questioned and mocked without mercy my resources of ingenuity and reason.

Such were Dorothy's thoughts, as she mentally asked him again, What *would* you have been able to tell me? The mouth of the dead man hung open a little in that terrible smile, as if to whisper that death had closed its ability to attain speech. In Dorothy's mind she saw the flesh as a livid green—not of decay but rather of some unearthly dissonance, a discord heard in this world as an echo, much imperfect, of a blast of sound from some other space.

2.

Dorothy's trombone playing tended to remind me of Charles Majid Greenlee's: she had that same graceful authority and strength in timbre, phrasing and imagination. Strange that an Art History postgraduate from London University should also be such a good jazz trombonist. We first met in New York, when I was going around clubs and bars in a search for the whereabouts of the legendary vocalist Patty Waters. Dorothy was playing with a group in one of the clubs; and for a while we played together in a quintet, although my prowess as a clarinettist certainly doesn't equal her own abilities.

From where I sat in the kitchen, drinking coffee, I could hear her playing that Ellington classic, 'Prelude to a Kiss'. Her playing—always reflective and strongly lyrical—today, unmistakably, had an inflection of melancholy, which I couldn't help connecting to her concern over the murder.

•

—Look at what I found in the house, she said, producing the copy of *Apocalypse* and opening it at the underlined passage. She sat down opposite me and lit a cigarette.—You must have thought this an important clue, I said.—Well, maybe, she replied.—But, I persisted, you *did* think it important enough to remove it from the house.—Yes, said Dorothy; you see, Benno, I've always liked van der Meer's writings on Christian art, and I don't have a copy of this book.

•

—What do the rooms afford us—?

—As evidence?

—Trace; track....

—On which to home in.

—Yes, said Dorothy; on which to home in.

We were examining the diagram she'd made of the house, and her notes regarding the various objects she'd found there. I asked her why she'd concerned herself to such an extent with what seemed to me the ordinary and even trivial paraphernalia of the murdered man's existence.

—They tell us about the sort of world he lived in, Benno. They're witnesses, and what they tell us may provide some understanding of why this crime occurred.

She smiled at me then; and I was struck anew by her

winningly intelligent and kindly eyes, and her open, sensuous smile. I'd always thought myself marvellously fortunate to have known this woman, however much hurt my hopeless love for her caused me.

My admiration precluded any attempt to dissuade her from investigating the mystery.

How useless it would have been to say, This isn't your concern, Dorothy; let the police deal with it. For a start, I knew that the preliminary investigation hadn't left her feeling overly impressed by their abilities. But I said anyway: Is it so important for you to find out, Dorothy? You hardly knew him.

—I'd only met him once, it's true, she said. It was at Rose and Arturo's, about six months ago. He'd already given up painting by that time. Rose and Arturo were practically the only people he ever saw; he'd been an almost total recluse for years. Then he telephoned me from that absurd, decaying, ramshackle house of his and asked me to meet him there—when I knew damn well *no one*—not even Rose or Arturo—had been invited there in over a year. Don't you think that he knew something was going to happen? And that he wanted me to help him, or to share his terror, or at least to *know* about it?

—Rose and Arturo were away, she went on, and when he found he couldn't reach them, he must have remembered me and decided he'd have to take a chance on someone he barely knew at all. But he *did* take that chance—and I can't ignore that. By the way—I *do* think the van der Meer book may give us a clue of some sort.

I laughed.—Well, I said, I did *wonder* if you'd been kidding about taking it because you didn't already have a copy.

—And the objects, she said. You know, he was still arranging those bottles and vases and glass balls and things in the same way as when he used to paint them. But as far as anyone knows, he quit painting at least a year ago.

—Couldn't he just have left them like that from the last time he did paint them? I asked.—I thought of that, she answered, but he wasn't the sort of person who simply left things around. He was too careful and tidy, however much he let that house of his fall to pieces around him without trying to fix it up at all.

—What connection do you make between the passage in the book, I asked, and the fact that he was still arranging those things as if he were going to paint them?

Dorothy stood up and shook back her blond hair from her eyes.—Let me think about it a little more, she said, and walked off into the next room. In a minute I heard her playing the first bars of Monk's 'Round Midnight'. I put the kettle on to make another cup of coffee.

3.

It was only a couple of days later that Dorothy received a phone-call from her friend Rose, who had just come back from a holiday in France to the "news" that the painter Geoffrey Johnston had been murdered.

Dorothy briefly gave the details of what had happened: the phone-call she'd received from Geoffrey; her visit to the house and discovery of his corpse; and the shadowy figure she'd caught sight of in the room. She also told Rose the results of the preliminary police investigation, and mentioned her own tentative—and so far fruitless—attempts to find out why the painter had been killed.

—I'd like to come over sometime soon and talk with you again about Geoffrey and his work, Dorothy said.

—I don't think anything I can say will be of any assistance in trying to discover a motive, Dorothy. Geoff had no enemies that I know of. He wasn't connected with any secret organisations—or if he was, it was a secret to me. And he wasn't wealthy.

—But of course, she continued, you know I'm always happy to see you, and I certainly don't mind telling you whatever I can. By the way, I have some journal-notes that Geoffrey left with me; he seemed to attach a certain importance to them—in as much as he asked me to keep them safe for him.

—Would it be all right for me to look at them? asked Dorothy.

—Yes, I'm sure it's all right. Poor Geoff, he was such a harmless soul. God knows why anyone would kill him. But I *don't* think I'll be of any help, Dorothy. And the notes he left with me are just some private musings.

—Well, I'd like to see them just the same. When could I come by? This afternoon?

—No, you'd better make it tomorrow. After three.

—Fine, said Dorothy. I'll see you tomorrow.

•

Dorothy's car was, as usual, being repaired; it was hardly ever available for use, but even when it was, it then often broke down while she was *en route*. So we waited, in a light rain, for a bus to take us to Rose and Arturo's. The bus stop was situated directly opposite a large public square, which featured a billboard-sized TV-screen and a nondescript abstract sculpture in yellow-painted metal. We were too far from the square to hear the TV clearly. The disjunctive appearance—the scale and the colour, in particular—of the televised images, in relation to the surrounding sights, gave a strangely dreamlike effect to the scene, an effect that was enhanced by the faint wash of sound.

The program being screened was from a children's educational series on modern artists; this particular episode was devoted to Marcel Duchamp. The format consisted of a number of cartoon sequences depicting various stages and aspects of Duchamp's career. Bemused and angry viewers were shown grouped around the *Nude Descending a Staircase No. 2* at the Armoury Show; after which we saw Duchamp selecting a bottle rack from a store, his act of will in choosing it being the medium of its insertion into an aesthetic context. Next, there was a sequence depicting the dust accumulating on the glass surface of *The Bride Stripped Bare by Her Bachelors, Even* (the dust "breeding", in Duchamp's metaphor), as it lay on trestles in his studio, Duchamp later sticking down some of the dust as a form of colouring. The program also showed Duchamp painting the Chocolate Grinder detail of *The Bride*, the "chocolate" in question being sperm, as Dorothy explained to me. (—Messy, she commented as we discussed this last image.) Later sequences showed Duchamp playing chess, having supposedly abandoned art; helping to realise a gallery environment by hanging coal sacks from the ceiling and making huge cobwebs out of miles of string; and secretly working on his last *opus, Etant donnés,* gathering bits of décor from the countryside and from building-yards.

Dorothy wondered about certain images they hadn't included. She thought of Duchamp with his hair soaped into horns in a photograph for the cover of a gambling method, and Duchamp in drag, photographed for the label of a perfume bottle: the endless theatrical flair so characteristic of the man (his art being a form of visual and intellectual theatre). She also thought of the desiccated, cadaverous face of the elderly Duchamp. She thought of his statement, "We are always alone: everybody by himself, like in a shipwreck." And she thought of Joseph Cornell's dream of engaging his services in finding Delacroix's handkerchief.

But I thought of a trip I'd made to Singapore once with two friends, who insisted on treating the pitiful conditions of the poor as an exotic spectacle that existed for their benefit; and of my angry outburst when I couldn't stand their attitude—their detachment, lack of care—any longer.

Arturo, whom I'd not met before, was a small, burly man, stylishly and formally dressed, with the greying hair brushed back off the broad forehead of his pudgy face, and calm, serious eyes. He had been the first person to really appreciate Geoffrey Johnston's paintings, and had helped to arrange his first exhibition. Johnston was already middle-aged at that time, and even then he was reclusive and unworldly. Apparently his contact with the art world had been depressing to him and had contributed not a little to his eventual abandonment of painting.

Rose—a petite woman with curly brown hair, bright eyes and a ready smile—remembered one occasion in particular which had seriously upset and obsessed Johnston. He'd been invited to a party by a composer, a man who in his youth had been in Paris in the '20s and '30s and had known many of the European artists of that time. Geoffrey hadn't usually accepted invitations to parties, but this man had promised to show him his collection of artworks, including things by Gris and Arp, and the temptation had been too great. Besides, Geoffrey was, according to Rose, a somewhat naïve, unsuspecting person, and he'd failed to take the measure of this man. (—A snake, Arturo added about the composer; a vicious reptile.) What Geoffrey gradually discovered was that the composer had invited people who hated one another, so that he could sit back and enjoy the spectacle of a series of nasty scenes. But Geoffrey couldn't understand why *he'd* been invited, as he had no enemies that he knew of. Then he found out who his enemy was: the composer himself. This man abused him maliciously in front of a group of his young hangers-on, but as Geoffrey insisted (and this was what really troubled him), there was absolutely no reason at all for the man to hate him. The abuse was empty— based on no understanding of the nature of Geoffrey's work or what Geoffrey believed in. The emptiness of it was, for Geoffrey, the really sinister part.

I asked if there was any possibility of this man having hated Johnston enough to have been involved in his murder, but Dorothy remarked that there wasn't any chance of that, for the bare reason that the man had died more than two years ago.

—Besides, added Rose, I think he'd lost interest in Geoff soon after the party. Geoff didn't rise to the bait very well; however offended he was, however shocked, he was unfailingly polite and dignified, and that bastard was after a very different sort of reaction. And he had plenty of other victims; Geoffrey hadn't been especially important to him.

Arturo broke in to say that he didn't want us to get the impression that all of Johnston's contacts with other artists had been of this type; it was an extreme example of a particular kind of experience. Geoffrey did complain a good deal about the pettiness, egotism and competitiveness of other artists, as well as the bitchiness of some of them; but there were others he liked and respected and would never have said a bad word about.

—Of course, he added, he liked my Rose, didn't he? He smiled at Rose, who smiled back affectionately.— And he liked your work, too, Arturo went on. He always told me that you were the only video artist he really did like.

—Perhaps, said Rose. He told me he thought it would be a good thing if I went into doing video therapy with disturbed kiddies!

We all laughed at this, and it was obvious that Rose had not been offended by the painter's suggestion.

Dorothy and I were invited to stay on for dinner, and while Dorothy continued to talk with Arturo about the painter, I went out to the kitchen to help Rose with her preparations. Unfortunately, we discovered that a bottled vinaigrette had a suspiciously musty smell to it, after I had already poured it liberally over the salad. I went out to buy a new bottle of vinaigrette, and when I got back Rose was washing the salad and trying to wipe the dressing off with bits of toilet paper. (—It's all I could find, she said apologetically.)

Throughout dinner and afterwards, we continued to talk about Geoffrey Johnston. Rose and Arturo reminisced about him at length, and it was plain that however eccentric and reclusive an individual he had been, they'd both been genuinely fond of him. They also talked about his interest in Christian mystical writings and the probable relevance of this to his work. Two things emerged from this discussion: firstly, the idea of the physical world as a text which could be read symbolically or hieroglyphically, with a good deal of emphasis on Johnston's part on such aspects or capacities of common things as those of receiving, containing, providing, veiling, showing, enduring, and so forth; secondly, the idea of an interrelatedness of phenomena in terms of some sort of transcendent order or unity. Arturo pointed out that Johnston had felt that these ideas were in direct opposition to the dominant world-views that reduced phenomena to the level of sheer, valueless matter for the manipulation of the will. Geoffrey tended to see innumerable negative features of the modern period—the post-modern, too—in a metaphysical light; and he would occasionally disclose some very pessimistic expectations about the increasing, and deepening, negativity of the immediate future. His paintings had been an attempt at realising some disclosure of that transcendent unity he believed in, and as such constituted a counter-force to the world-views on which he blamed so much. But apparently, towards the end, his pessimism about prevailing ideological tendencies and the accelerating violence and cynicism of the present, together with his dissatisfaction with the art world, had reduced him to silence. This was, at least, the only way Rose and Arturo were able to interpret the inactivity at the end of Geoffrey's life.

Finally, Dorothy reminded Rose of the manuscript she'd promised to show her. It consisted of a non-sequential arrangement of notes, which Dorothy found to be very roughly expressed thoughts about various subjects, and certainly of no direct relevance to the painter's death.

•

I cut myself off from the others, & have stopped altogether now. I couldn't be *seen* to be opposed—I've been judged as the *same* as what I dislike so thoroughly & which I judge to be so wrong. Yet I have nothing else: I can *do* nothing else.

I've sought everywhere, going from the most esteemed works to others that are scorned or ignored—from Cézanne to Len Crawford, from Ghyka to Wroblewski with his *Art Alphabet*, from Goethe to Swedenborg & even Peter John Olivi. I've gone to *whatever* was useful in my search.

In the beauty of a person's being we recognise the adumbration of eternal life—the beauty that transcends death & decay.

Grace, to build. The City: unity of things, beyond totalization (rule of numbers, quantification, levelling of differences & individual values). Relation is *via* the Absolute (infinity / eternity).

Fate & character: the earthly nexus providing an opening for the action of supernatural grace; or in other instances, providing an opposed contrast against which the realm of grace shines in manifestation.

The senses: mediational & instrumental (rather than essential).

They open their mouths & breathe out ignorance & egotism onto their canvases.

Then I saw an angel standing in the sun, & he cried aloud to all the birds flying in mid-heaven: "Come & gather for God's great supper, to eat the flesh of kings & commoners & fighting men, the flesh of horses & their riders, the flesh of all men, slave & free, great & small!" How would the angel make itself manifest to us? I often think: through 'the smallest of us.' The humblest; the least expected.

4.

There was a golden tone to the light, which seemed to guide the predominantly middle-class, smart-set people in their summer clothing into orderly groupings amongst the trees, like an updated seventeenth-century dream of classicism. The unbroken white nudity of a small girl's body swept dancing into a space of more intense light, the blank, numb tonality so intrusive, disturbing, that she might as well been a glacier suddenly introduced into the scene. She joined a group of other children, dancing around the seated or standing adults sipping tea and eating cake.

I had gone to the park to attend an open-air concert in which Dorothy was a participant. While waiting for it to begin, I tried to make friends with a good-natured labrador, feeding it cake-crumbs. Its owner, looking across at the rather sloppily dressed, shaggy-haired, hunchbacked young man who had accosted the unsuspecting animal, called her dog abruptly away.

Gradually the musicians assembled for the concert: a fairly large group, with a female vocalist, saxophones doubling flute or clarinet, brass, electric piano, bass and drums. I was greatly surprised, when Dorothy appeared and came over to greet me; in as much as I discovered she was playing bass trumpet instead of trombone for this occasion.

The high-point of the concert—for me, at least—was during the rendition of 'What Are You Doing the Rest of Your Life'. Dorothy stood up and performed a standout solo, every note possessing a beautiful and tender gravity, and firmly assured in its placing. At the end of the solo, where I anticipated the line to be resolved into a final tone or two, it unexpectedly continued in an upward-thrusting, sustained burst of notes. I thought of Coltrane's playing at the end of 'Meditations', but equally of Heinrich Schütz's wonderful cantata for tenor voice, 'Eile, mich, Gott, zu erretten'.

And at the very end came another surprise, for the band played a fine, limpid arrangement of Erik Satie's 'Gymnopédies No.1', with its modest, graceful melody-line sung to the following words:

The spinning shadows falling are like
the threads of our life
and they become the threads of our love
(threads knotting our love).
The circle's haze of movement is circles-
within-circles when you have entered the Dance –
when at the heart you have kissed the lips of
the Queen of the Dance.

I remarked afterwards to Dorothy that if the 'Gymnopédies' was obviously the work of a young man (Satie having been in his early twenties), those words were just as obviously the work of someone even more youthful. She smiled at me.—You're right, Benno, she said; the young man who wrote them is, I believe, not more than eighteen.

5.

Dorothy was on her way back from the library, where she'd been trying to do some research for an article on Ruskin. Her nerves were strained by anxiety over her other research, into Geoffrey Johnston's death, and she had made little progress on the piece. She stopped off at a café for some chocolate cake and coffee; but her attention was forcibly drawn to a conversation at the next table between a young man and woman, both of whom (it transpired) had just been released from a mental hospital. From discussing different possibilities of committing suicide, their conversation turned to the necessity, as the man saw it, of "eliminating" sectors of society for the good—if not of society as a whole—of people like himself, who had the correct ideas and the will to carry them out. He assured his companion that, although he hadn't started to "eliminate" people yet, he would begin by killing someone soon.—What sort of people would you get rid of? she asked.—Oh, he said, the inadequates; then the queers, and the Yids, and the niggers.

At that point, Dorothy lost her temper. She got up suddenly and, turning to the pair, thrust the table into the man's abdomen, and then before he could recover she punched him several times in the face while his companion looked on in paralysed disbelief. Dorothy turned on her heel and walked out of the café; she was several yards up the road before she remembered that she had neglected to pay her bill.

•

We met in the Tate and walked around the Turner galleries, Dorothy quoting for my benefit Ruskin's censured remark, that Turner "was sent as a prophet of God to reveal to men the mysteries of His universe, standing, like the great angel of the Apocalypse, clothed with a cloud...." Geoffrey Johnston's calm, lucid portrayals of mundane objects were a long way from Turner's visions of cataclysm and apocalyptic light; but the apocalyptic note in Johnston—his belief that the disclosure of spiritual vision or truth exerts a counterforce to the accelerating powers of subterfuge, deceit and violence—was indeed the light by which we now understood his project as a painter.

Adjourning to the coffee bar (which Dorothy particularly liked for the chocolate cake they served), we discussed the melancholy persistence which had, presumably, kept the painter's sight fixed on his collection of objects and their arrangement, even after he'd stopped painting them. So much had been concentrated upon them, as a sort of microcosm, with their symbolic properties and potentialities waiting to be explored, expressed. We both now spoke—I realised—with a note of affection for the painter; he'd come to haunt our thoughts and speech, enlivening them with his absence.

—Benno! said Dorothy; it's no use going on—I've failed. I've done nothing to solve the crime. I've failed him.

Tears began to run down her cheeks and the sides of her nose.

•

Sky's blood-flow.

Imagine an open hand raised with the palm outwards. And the other hand, slightly below it, clamped around the upper length of a sword-handle, the massive blade of the sword rising above the head with its strangely gentle, calm eyes.

Imagine, too, a voice....

Dorothy and I were in her flat, practising a two-part arrangement of Luiz Bonfa's 'Manhã de Carnaval', when we were interrupted by the telephone.

It was Donald Wilson, an art-historian friend of Dorothy's. His voice was trembling and he had barely said hello when he blurted out: As one Christian to another, Dorothy, I had nothing to do with Pamela's disappearance—nothing!

Dorothy got him to calm down a little and tell her what had happened, and certain details began to emerge: he had been having an affair with a student of his, and after a violent quarrel she had disappeared, her room being vacant for days now, the floor littered with bloody bandages. He had looked everywhere for her, without finding any clue. Dorothy suggested it was a case for the police; but Wilson flew into such a panic at this that she knew she would have to go and talk with him, at least.

Having promised to see him immediately, she replaced the receiver.—Benno, how do you feel about our taking on another case? she asked.

THE DOROTHY AND BENNO STORIES: *BLUES FOR PAMELA*

Chapter One

1.

Dorothy and Benno were rehearsing in Dorothy's flat, working out a two-part arrangement of the Luiz Bonfá composition, 'Manhã de Carnaval'. Dorothy played the melody on trombone, with Benno adding a clarinet obbligato, keeping to a conversational and almost hushed feeling—well suited to the tender character of the composition. The inspiration for the arrangement came partly from a Sandy Bull recording of the piece, and partly from Lee Konitz and Marshall Brown's unusually thoughtful rendition of 'Strutting with Some Barbecue'. It was a perfect vehicle for Dorothy, with her reflective, "inward" way of playing.

They were interrupted by a telephone-call from Donald Wilson, an art-historian friend of Dorothy's. (He and Dorothy had pursued post-graduate studies at the Courtauld Institute at the same time.) He had barely said hello, before he blurted out: As one Christian to another, Dorothy, I swear I had nothing to do with Pamela's disappearance—nothing! Dorothy got him to calm down, and gradually it emerged from what he told her that he'd been having an affair with a student of his, and after a violent quarrel she had vanished, her room littered with bloody bandages. He had searched everywhere he could think of, without finding any clue to her whereabouts. When Dorothy suggested that it was a case for the police, Wilson flew into such a panic that she knew she would have to see him, at least. Having promised to make her way over to his place immediately, she replaced the receiver.

—Benno, she said, how do you feel about our taking on another case?

2.

Dorothy and Benno had only just concluded—or failed to conclude, depending on how you look at it—their first case. They had investigated the murder of an artist named Geoffrey Johnston; and if the discovery of either a motive or a murderer had failed to materialise, they had been successful in another investigation, which took over from their original quest. That is to say, they had found themselves deeply involved in an investigation of the creative and spiritual ideas that lay behind Geoffrey Johnston's work as a painter.

3.

Buridan's Ass:

They placed food and water at equal distances from
the ass, and he died of hunger and thirst between
them, unable to choose between eating or drinking
first.

Dorothy handed the note to Benno, shaking back the
blond hair from her eyes in a characteristic gesture.—
It's in Pamela Cotman's handwriting, she said; Donald
found it on her desk after she disappeared.

Benno looked up from the note, into Dorothy's
keenly intelligent and searching eyes. He felt helpless.—
You think it means anything? he ventured at last.

—I think it's a parable about the advantages of
making some kind of choice over failing to make a
choice, said Dorothy. She lit a cigarette.—What do you
think about that as an interpretation? she asked.

—Sure, said Benno. Sounds OK to me. But where
does it lead us?

—I don't know yet, said Dorothy. Donald told
me that Pamela had been upset or anxious about
something, but he didn't have any idea what it was; he

said their quarrel was probably not a significant factor in her disappearance. (She'd become very angry about the fact that he'd given her a low grade on one of her art history essays.) Nor did he know what the note referred to.

—So what's our next step? asked Benno.

—You'll have to let me think about it a little, she said, getting up from the table and walking into the next room. She began playing Billy Strayhorn's classic ballad, 'Lush Life'. Benno put the kettle on to make himself some coffee.

4.

Benno took it upon himself to pay a call on Donald Wilson. It was not that he didn't trust Dorothy to find out the facts of the case for herself—if anything, Benno's admiration for Dorothy, springing from hopeless love, precluded even the slightest doubt regarding her capabilities. Rather, Benno felt left out of things, and wanted to be able to say he had done *something* towards solving the mystery of Pamela Cotman's disappearance; even if it was only to repeat what Dorothy had already done.

He had phoned Wilson to let him know he was coming by. As he walked from the station to Wilson's house, he hummed 'Moon, Don't Come Up Tonight', and then 'Goodbye Pork Pie Hat'. Benno located the house, and rang Donald Wilson's doorbell. Presently a light came on in the hallway, and Benno saw a looming, shadowy figure through the glass, advancing to the door. He soon found himself looking at a tall, broad-shouldered man with a crisp black beard. Wilson had genial but sad eyes, and his mouth crinkled into a rather weary smile.

—Benno Lieberman, said Benno.—Ah, said Donald Wilson, I've been expecting you. Come in, Benny.—It's *Benno*, said Benno indignantly (he hated people getting his name wrong, as they often did). Wilson seemed not to have heard him; instead of answering, he silently led Benno up a flight of stairs and into his flat.

—Sit down, Benny, said Wilson. Would you like a drink of some sort?

—Vodka, if you have it, said Benno. And it's *Benno*.

While Donald Wilson was in the kitchen getting their drinks, Benno looked through Wilson's record collection: as sure an index to a person's character as Benno could conceive. Wilson's interests ranged from Mozart to Eartha Kitt; but Benno was disconcerted to find he had no Charlie Parker or John Coltrane, no Miles Davis or Don Cherry, no Sidney Bechet or Lee Konitz; in fact, no jazz at all. Benno could only think that Wilson kept the jazz records somewhere else in the flat.

When Wilson returned, Benno asked: What instrument do you play, Don?

—Actually, said Wilson, I don't, Benny.

—You don't play an instrument, huh, said Benno. Well, tell me, Don, where do you keep your jazz records?

—I'm afraid I don't have any. Oh, wait a minute: I

do have a Herb Alpert record. Yes, that's right. I guess that's jazz of some sort, isn't it?

—No jazz records, huh, said Benno.

—Perhaps you'd like to hear some Herb Alpert while we talk, suggested Wilson.

—Thanks, Don, said Benno, but some other time. Let's get straight down to business. Have you thought of anything that might be of help since you spoke to Dorothy yesterday? Anything—however small it might be—that seemed unusual to you about your girlfriend's behaviour before her disappearance. Or anything else that she left in her flat that may help us.

—I take it you haven't made much of that note? asked Donald Wilson.

—We're working on it, Don, said Benno.

—Well, there is one thing. A short time—just a couple of weeks—before she disappeared, Pamela had spent a few days in Boulogne, visiting an elderly novelist named Georges Gorin. She'd been corresponding with him for a while, as an admirer of his writings, and Gorin had suggested that she pay him a visit at his home. After her return, Pamela seemed changed—she was withdrawn and troubled.

—This could be important, Don, said Benno. Did

she say anything about what happened when she stayed with this guy?

—No, she didn't. I thought that was rather strange—don't you?

—Uh huh, said Benno. Could be something in this, Don. Do you happen to know this Gorin's address?

—I don't, Benny, but you could reach him through his publisher—I'll jot the address down for you.

—Fine, said Benno. This may be a good clue, Don.

Wilson presently handed him a slip of paper with the address, and Benno got up to leave.—If you think of anything else, give us a call, he said.

5.

Dorothy wrote a letter to Georges Gorin and sent it by way of his Paris publisher. A week later she received the following reply:

> Dear Dorothy Evans,
>
> Thank you kindly for your letter. I think we could better discuss things if you came here and stayed for a couple of days or so. You would be very welcome. Bring your friend along, if you like. I already have one house-guest at the moment—a young woman from Australia, who is engaged upon a PhD thesis on my writings—but there is plenty of room. I would suggest you come next Friday—there is a ferry in the early afternoon.
>
> Yours sincerely,
>
> Georges Gorin.

Dorothy couldn't make up her mind whether she should go or not. Why couldn't Gorin tell her in a letter whatever he knew that was relevant? Why did she and Benno have to go all the way to Boulogne to find out?

She decided to see her younger sister, Millie. Millie could always be counted on for sound advice. At this time in the evening, she'd usually be found in a certain gymnasium across the street from where she lived. (Millie had chosen her home because of its location near the gym.) Unlike Dorothy she had no practical interest in music, but instead had dedicated herself to bodybuilding. Millie had what someone once described as "not just muscle but 'muscle muscle'"; her physique had even been compared to that of the legendary Suzy Green.

Millie was performing French curls when Dorothy located her. Even though Dorothy secretly harboured a wish that her sister would give up pumping iron and learn the saxophone (or any other instrument, for that matter), she felt a sort of family pride in the determination and success with which Millie had pursued her interest in "physical culture".

With Dorothy's arrival, Millie quit her training for the evening and took Dorothy back to her flat for some coffee.

—I've started on a new case, said Dorothy.

—What, after the Geoff Johnston fiasco? said Millie.

—Forget about that, Millie.

—Beginner's bad luck, huh? said Millie.

—Listen, said Dorothy, lighting a cigarette; Benno and I –

—You're not *still* hanging out with that creep, are you? interrupted her sister.

—Just *listen* for a minute! Dorothy said.

—Look, honey—no need to fly off the handle. Hey, you're looking a bit peaked, kid. How long is it since you've taken a holiday?

—As it happens, answered Dorothy, I've just been invited to Boulogne. I was about to ask you what you thought about my going.

—Honey, I'm sure it's just what you need.

—Thanks, Millie, said Dorothy. I knew I could count on you for advice.

—Any time, honey. Any time.

Chapter Two.

1.

After getting lost several times, they found George Gorin's house, in a small and pleasant street not far from the central part of the town. They rang the doorbell, and after a short time a small, grey-haired man with a florid face appeared. He opened his mouth and then closed it again, looking intently at his visitors and seemingly undecided whether to say anything to them. Dorothy and Benno stood waiting. He opened his mouth again, and this time he spoke the words: I take it you're Dorothy Evans.—Yes, said Dorothy, relieved at his having broken the silence; and this is my friend Benno Lieberman. Gorin adjusted his glasses, scrutinised Benno and Dorothy very intently again, and then turned and walked back inside. Benno shot Dorothy a troubled look.—I think he means for us to follow him, she whispered.—Well, he might *tell* us, Benno whispered back.

If he had proved distinctly taciturn to begin with, Gorin became flamboyantly expansive as time wore on. He led them into the dining room and offered them some anisette.—I'm absolutely addicted to it, he confessed to

43

them, pouring himself a large drink of the liqueur. He also offered them bread and paté, explaining that they would have dinner later in the evening, when his other guest, Laura Jameson, returned from her sightseeing.— Charming girl, he said of Laura; I'm sure you'll both like her.

—Are you a musician? asked Gorin, commenting on Dorothy's instrument-case. Dorothy admitted to being a jazz trombonist, although, she said, she had never intended a career in music.

In fact, it was through a peculiar set of circumstances that she began playing professionally. When she was at university, she organised a series of jazz concerts at her college. On one occasion, the band that she'd booked went missing a short while before the concert. Their manager telephoned her and asked if she could help him locate them, suggesting that they would probably be at one public bar or another that they tended to frequent—and he dictated a list of addresses to her. The members of the band, she explained, were notorious for hard drinking, and for not turning up to gigs unless they were (so to speak) chaperoned; they were, however, excellent musicians. She managed to find them, but they were without their trombonist, and had no idea of his whereabouts. Before she knew what was happening, Dorothy heard herself telling them that *she* played trombone. Although the band members were a little sceptical at first, when they actually heard her play (and she said that she trembled the whole time that she auditioned for them), they decided to let her "sub" for the missing trombonist. The concert was a success, and one of the musicians—a drummer named Bob Clark—told her that her playing reminded him of the great Charles Majid Greenlee. When it turned out that the missing trombonist had permanently disappeared (no one was ever sure what had happened to him), she was offered a place in the band, and even travelled to New York with the other musicians during the following summer vacation.

Gorin listened to this story with visible interest.—I suppose you like Charlie Parker's playing? he asked her.—Yes, very much, said Dorothy, while Benno nodded agreement.—*Poor* Charlie Parker, said Gorin. *Such* a sad life. *What?!* I knew him, in Paris, he continued, and sat back to see what effect this statement had on his guests. As they looked suitably awed (*Really?* said Benno), he launched into an anecdote about how one of his other friends, Jean-Paul Sartre, had wanted to meet Parker, so Gorin had brought them together. They'd met at a café in Montparnasse, and Gorin had said to Parker:

Bird, I want you to meet Jean-Paul Sartre.—Pleased to meet you, man, said Parker; I've got all your records at home—I've admired your playing for years. —He thought, continued Gorin, that Sartre was *yet another* French jazz musician who wanted to meet him. *Poor Jean-Paul Sartre. What?!*

Georges Gorin, as it turned out, had known everybody, practically, who was famous in the arts. Dorothy and Benno were soon treated to anecdotes about W. H. Auden, James Joyce, Jean Arp, Yves Klein, Paul Eluard, Igor Stravinsky, and many others. It was a ceaseless flow of gossip, with at times a mischievous quality, punctuated by exclamations of *What?!* and accompanied by a good deal of drinking.

It was also punctuated by the arrival of Laura Jameson, a tiny, very slender woman in her early twenties, with a long, thin face, high cheekbones, an extremely large mouth, and long plaits; she spoke with a pronounced Australian accent; and when asked if she played an instrument, she had to answer in the negative. But Gorin let nothing stop him for more than a brief pause. He prepared their dinner while shouting out anecdotes from the kitchen.

Coming back into the dining room to get another drink, Gorin began whistling what was recognisably a blues melody, rather rudimentary in character.—What's the tune, Georges? asked Benno.—That, replied Gorin, is the melody of the only blues written by Franz Kafka. *Poor* Kafka. I knew him in Berlin, in 1923; I was seventeen at the time. Of course, he died the following year.

—Kafka wrote a *blues?* said Dorothy, incredulously.

—Oh, Kafka loved blues, said Gorin. He had the best collection of blues records in Berlin.

—Isn't that impossible? said Dorothy.

Gorin looked puzzled.—Do you know of someone who had a *better* collection? he asked.

—No, said Dorothy, I meant I shouldn't have thought he could have had a blues collection at all.

Gorin looked shocked.—You think Franz Kafka was a *liar?* he asked.

Dorothy retreated into acquiescence.—No, Georges, she said; of course not. Would you tell us the words of his song?

—Better than that, he said, I'll sing them for you. *What?!* He cleared his throat, and began to sing. He had a thin, old man's voice, but he still managed to bring a considerable amount of gusto to his performance.

You keep moving, but the Law'll be coming around,
Keep moving, yes, that Law'll be coming around,
You've done nothing, but the Law'll throw you down.

Dorothy quickly unpacked her trombone, and joined in.

It's a dirty pity, and it's a crying shame,
It's a dirty pity, low down crying shame,
The way the Law will hold a man to blame.

Woke up one morning, with detectives standing by,
Woke up one morning, with detectives standing by,
I'll die an accused man, you know I wouldn't lie.

The meal that followed mainly consisted of fillet of sole and salad. The fish reminded Benno of an odd and amusing incident in his life which—not wishing to be left behind in the telling of anecdotes—he decided to recount to the others. Sometime late in 1972, he had visited the elderly poet and painter David Jones at a Catholic nursing home in Harrow. They had spent several hours talking about a great variety of subjects—Jones' art-school days, his admiration for Georges Braque (which Benno shared), his relationship to Eric Gill, and a host of other things. Before Benno had realised what time it was he found himself present at Jones' evening meal, which was brought in by one of the nuns. The main course was some kind of fish, which was obviously not to David Jones' taste. He asked Benno to hand him a waste-paper basket; when Benno did so, he threw the fish into it. —Don't want to hurt their feelings by leaving it on the plate, he said.

To Benno's relief, the story was a success with his host and Laura (Dorothy had heard it before). Gorin expressed surprise, however, that Benno had visited David Jones. (As Benno had so far said very little— and nothing at all that didn't relate to jazz—Gorin wondered what his interest in David Jones could have been. Perhaps Jones was a collector of Bix Beiderbecke records; or had he played banjo in a band performing New Orleans jazz?)—Oh, said Benno airily, I'd known various of his paintings since my early teens, and I came across his collection of essays, *Epoch and Artist*, when I was eighteen, and that interested me a great deal. A couple of years later I started reading the poetry also. And then I became friendly with a magazine editor who knew Jones, and that prompted my decision to visit him.

—You hide your light under a bushel, Benno, said Georges Gorin. *What?!*

Benno looked a little put out by this remark at first, but when Dorothy gave in to the laughter she'd been attempting to suppress, he shrugged his shoulders and then smiled.

2.

—You kids get through a lot of drinking, said Georges Gorin, meaning *drink* (he eyed his depleted bottles of anisette and cognac).

Benno and Dorothy—thirty-two and thirty-five respectively, hence much older than the expression "kids" would generally convey—looked at each other sheepishly.

Perhaps with the idea of conserving his alcohol supply, Gorin took his three guests, late in the evening, to a café near the quay, packed out with night-owl teenagers, to chat and drink coffee. When Dorothy had gone to order more coffee and buy cigarettes, Gorin said to Benno, She's charming, isn't she?

Benno smiled in agreement; then he remembered something he'd been meaning to ask Gorin since their arrival.

—Georges, he said, what instrument do you play?

3.

Sometime shortly after getting to sleep, Benno woke up again and proceeded to cough violently; he continued in this way, with small respite, until morning.

When Dorothy came to say good morning, she found an exhausted and miserable Benno. Benno was used to the fact that he was vulnerable to sudden colds; as a result, he was annoyed, but not anxious, about being kept awake most of the night with a hacking cough—which fortunately had now become less constant.

Dorothy went downstairs and announced to Gorin and Laura, who were about to begin their breakfast, that her friend had taken ill. When she went back upstairs to see if she could do anything for Benno, Gorin turned to Laura and said: *Poor* Benno Lieberman. And *what* a pity he's a hunchback.

4.

When at midday Benno finally emerged from his room, after managing to sleep for a few hours, he was feeling rested and in much better spirits. Having missed breakfast, he looked forward to a good lunch.

The others were sitting in the dining room, smoking and drinking coffee. Georges Gorin was holding forth on Asian religion and art, drawing on a trip he'd made to Japan for examples of what he felt to be the "minor" nature of Asian art, and criticising those Westerners who attached themselves to Asiatic religions when, in his opinion, they'd be better off coming to terms with their own religious traditions.

He stopped to acknowledge Benno's arrival (Dorothy and Laura both asking solicitously after Benno's health). The interruption enabled Dorothy to remark on Simone Weil's observation that Asian and Occidental art can be shown to have many corresponding features— such as the use of void space in both Chinese painting (especially of the Song period) and in Giotto; and that parallels can also be traced between Daoist thought on the one hand and Greek and Christian thinking on the other.

—Ah, said Gorin; *poor* Simone Weil.

—You didn't happen to know her? asked Benno.

—We met briefly, he said, in Paris—sometime in 1938. Terribly neurotic, of course. I remember a friend of mine kissed her, in a playful spirit, and she burst out crying.

—Did you get a chance to talk with her? asked Dorothy.

—A little, he said. The poet Joë Bousquet put me in touch with Simone. He probably thought we'd have things in common because we were both Jewish. *What?!*

—Of course, continued Gorin, Simone was hostile to the Jewish tradition, to the extent of thinking that Christianity had more in common with Greek spirituality.

—You wouldn't have agreed about much, in that case? asked Dorothy, who had already become aware that Georges Gorin took his Jewishness very seriously.

—No, said Gorin, not much. In fact, he said after a pause, in which he helped himself to another of Dorothy's cigarettes, we didn't agree about anything.

While Gorin and Dorothy were conversing about Simone Weil, Benno had poured himself some coffee from a jug. He wondered at what time Gorin would serve lunch. As it turned out, however, his hopes were shattered when Gorin did announce lunch an hour later. Gorin simply told Benno he wasn't well enough to eat anything and that was that. Benno walked out of the room in disgust and went back upstairs.

5.

Laura and Dorothy went for a walk together while Georges Gorin worked on his new novel.

Dorothy talked about her experience of living briefly in New York, while playing with the band; she added that it had been in New York that she'd met Benno.

—I do like Benno, said Laura, but I suspect he's a woman-hater.

—Well, *I've* never thought he was a woman-hater, said Dorothy. What a strange thing to say.

—Most men are, you know, said Laura. They feel castrated by women. And besides, Benno is gay, isn't he?

—Actually, no, said Dorothy.

—Really? said Laura, looking thoughtful. I felt certain he would be. But please don't think that I don't like your friend, even if he *is* boring. Boring people, after all, are really interesting.

—No, she said, I'm sorry, Laura, but boring people are really boring and interesting people are really interesting. And *I* don't find Benno boring, not in the least!

—*Oh*, said Laura, showing alarm at Dorothy's obvious impatience with her, *you don't understand* –

—What's there to not understand? said Dorothy, losing her temper. You've talked a lot of nonsense and been insulting about my friend.

Laura looked completely flustered.—But I *do* like Benno, she said helplessly.

They walked on in silence for a while. Then Dorothy took pity on Laura, and asked her to talk about her thesis on Georges Gorin. The rest of the afternoon passed uneventfully, and they were making their way back to Gorin's when they encountered Benno in the street.

—I didn't expect to come across you, said Dorothy, laughing; I thought you'd be resting.

Benno gave her an angry look.—I want to talk with you, he said—alone, if you don't mind.

Laura excused herself and walked away, even more convinced, no doubt, that Benno was a woman-hating homosexual.

—What's wrong? asked Dorothy.

—You deserted me! said Benno. You never asked me if I wanted to come with you—you just took off and left me to it. And I've had nothing to eat all day—I'm *starving*. I came out to find a restaurant, but you know I don't speak any French, so what's the use of my going into one when I won't be able to order anything.

—Benno, you're being rather melodramatic, said Dorothy. I thought you were too ill to come for a walk. Georges didn't give you lunch for the same reason—though I admit I thought it unnecessary for him to do that.

When Benno didn't reply, she added: We could go to a restaurant now, if you like. My French is a little rusty, but I can get by with it.

Benno cheered up enormously at the prospect of a meal. However, they managed to lose their way in trying to find a suitable eating-place, and ended up on the outskirts of the town before they realised their mistake. Feeling tired, they stopped first at a small café for a coffee; soon afterwards, they found a restaurant to their liking, where they had a large and leisurely meal. Dorothy insisted on a course of oysters; she was especially fond of them, and had been trying for years to get Benno (who had little interest in seafood) to try them; on this occasion he succumbed.

—Dorothy, said Benno, let's return to London as soon as we can. I've had enough of this place.

—You know, I think I have as well, she replied.

They arrived back at Gorin's shortly after Gorin and Laura had finished their evening meal. Dorothy apologised for their absence, saying that they'd gone for a walk and had lost their way. When Gorin suggested he reheat the remaining chicken casserole for them, they felt it impossible—from courtesy, and a desire to hide the fact that they'd already eaten—to refuse his kindness. He also insisted that they have bread and paté; and, as usual, there was plenty of coffee and alcohol. Sadly, it was an effort to hide the reluctance with which they partook of the meal.

Sometime during the repast, Dorothy announced their decision to leave on the early morning boat.

Now it was Gorin's turn to be melodramatic.— Benno will never get back alive, he said.

—Nevertheless, said Dorothy; we're going.

—Besides, added Gorin, if you expect me to come down to the quay to say goodbye at half-past one in the morning, you're expecting too much.

—We have to get back to London for a rehearsal, lied Benno.

—You're not well enough to travel, said Gorin, and then reiterated: You'll die on the boat.

Their determination won out over Gorin's insistence in the end. The evening's conversation took on a tone of farewell. Laura exchanged addresses with Dorothy and Benno, promising to send them whatever details she could find of current jazz activities in Australia.

Gorin launched expansively into a series of bizarre anecdotes about gay taxi-drivers in Tokyo. After a time Benno left the room (Dorothy presumed he had gone to his room to rest for a while). Laura decided to retire.

—Take care, my dear, she said to Dorothy, kissing her on the cheek, and then went to look for Benno to say goodbye.

Gorin and Dorothy spent the next hour drinking cognac together and talking about such diverse matters as the effect of ageing on the sexual appetites (Gorin) and the early playing of Lee Konitz (Dorothy).

Suddenly, in the middle of describing Brice Marden's recent exhibition at the Whitechapel Gallery, Dorothy stopped speaking and reached into the pocket of her leather coat; she brought out the slip of paper on which Pamela Cotman had written her note about "Buridan's Ass" and handed it to Gorin. All the distractions—the endless conversations and the drinking—of the past day and a half blew away; this, after all, was what they had come here for.

—Does that mean anything to you, Georges? she asked.

—John Buridan was a Scholastic philosopher, replied Gorin. The parable about the ass is always attributed to him, although in fact it doesn't appear in his surviving writings. *What?!*

—But what's the meaning of it? insisted Dorothy.

—It's to do with free will, he replied. The ass doesn't have the freedom to make a choice between the one equal need and the other. It's not a very realistic example, of course—*what?!* But a human being has the ability to choose—that's the upshot of the parable.

—That note is in Pamela's hand, said Dorothy.

—*Poor* Pamela Cotman, said Gorin. I don't doubt that it is. That parable sums up the poor girl's problem very well.

—What problem? asked Dorothy. What are you talking about?

—I'd been wondering when you were going to ask me about Pamela, said Georges Gorin. It's simple, really. She told me that she was in love with two men. She spoke of them both in a very idealised way. But she was caught between these two loves in such a way that she found it impossible to go on loving either of the men; because while loving one of them she also loved the other. Nor, even if it had been convenient (and it wasn't), would she have been able to love them together, for she felt she must give all her love to one or the other; and she couldn't. So she loved both of them, and yet was unable to love either.

—One of them was your friend Wilson, he continued; I don't know who the other man was—she never mentioned his name.

—Donald said she appeared changed after her visit here, said Dorothy. What do you make of that?

—*Poor* Donald Wilson, said Gorin. Too insensitive to see that the girl was in trouble until the problem had come to a head. *What?!*

—So you're saying that Pamela saw herself as deprived of the ability to choose one man or the other? That her will was paralysed by the situation she found herself in?

—No, not quite. Human beings are capable of tragic choice, as well. If Pamela hasn't killed herself (and I'm afraid it's quite possible that she has), then I imagine she's living alone in some place where she won't easily be found. I'm speaking, of course, from the knowledge I gathered of her, and from my intuition.

—Well, Georges, said Dorothy, that's very sad; but you've been a great help. I'm going to find Benno, she continued, getting up and walking towards the door, and let him know what you've told me.

Climbing the stairs, she looked at her watch and discovered they only had a half-hour until the boat sailed; they would have to quickly pack their things and then leave the house without further delay.

Dorothy knocked on Benno's door. A groggy voice said, Mmn?

—It's me, said Dorothy.

—Oh, come in, he replied in the same thick, unsteady voice.

She found him lying in bed, his face colourless and covered in sweat.

—Benno! exclaimed Dorothy. Whatever's wrong with you?

—It was those bloody oysters, said Benno. I've been sick *so* many times—*and* I've had diarrhoea.

—Well, she said, it's plain enough that we won't be leaving tonight.

—No, said Benno; I'm afraid we won't.

—Never mind. Let's hope you're well enough to leave in the morning. Can I get you anything?

—A cup of tea would be nice, said Benno.

She went back to the dining room and explained

the situation to their host, and without neglecting to mention her friend's request.

—It wouldn't be good for his stomach, said Gorin. Hot milk, *that's* what he needs.

So Benno was taken a cup of hot milk, which, as it happened, was something he absolutely detested.

That night Dorothy had a strange dream (which she was later able to relate to a memory of an old folk-ballad). She dreamt that she and Benno were medieval minstrels, who chanced upon the corpse of a drowned girl. They made a harp from her tresses and breastbone, and took the sad, grisly instrument with them when invited to play at her father's castle. When Dorothy set the harp on her knee, the strings began to sound by themselves; the ghostly tones were like a voice, a voice that distinctly shaped the words: My sister murdered me.

The latter part of the dream was not, Dorothy felt, in any way relevant; yet as a whole it seemed to her—however irrationally—a confirmation that Pamela was likely to be dead.

In the morning, when Dorothy looked in to see how he was, Benno told her about Laura's coming to see him the night before. He had just returned from the bathroom when she knocked on his door; he was pouring with sweat, and had forgotten to zip up his trousers. Laura was clearly embarrassed, and tried hard not to look in the direction of his fly.—It's been nice meeting you, Benno, she told him.—I'll write to you, he said.

Chapter Three.

It was some five months after Dorothy and Benno's stay in Boulogne that Georges Gorin visited London. During this time, there had been no discoveries about Pamela's fate. Dorothy invited Gorin to her flat, to have dinner with her and Benno.

—I've written some music about Pamela Cotman, Dorothy told him. It's called 'Blues for Pamela'. Shall I play it for you?

The piece was based on a contrast between slow, grave, quiet passages in the middle register descending into the lower register, and clusters of quavering arpeggios ending in falsetto-like tones, in some degree resembling bursts of passionate bird-song. Dorothy used this contrast both as a constructive device and as a dramatic effect—which she pursued sensitively and with ingenuity.

Her performance was applauded by Benno and Georges Gorin.

Benno asked Gorin, while they were having a pre-dinner drink, if Laura had been in touch recently.

—*Poor* Laura Jameson, said Gorin. Terrible case of arrested development. *What?!*

—Have you heard from her? asked Benno.

—Laura disappeared over two months ago, replied
Georges Gorin.

THE DOROTHY AND BENNO STORIES: *NIGHTMARE*

Millie lay still for a moment, listening to her own breathing, gradually becoming aware of the sounds beyond the door, and slowly coming back to where she was. She remembered yesterday's long freeway drive—the radio's music; the drumming of the tires on the sections; finally, the Santa Monica Turn-off and her first glimpse of the Pacific Ocean.

She eased out of bed and put on her dressing gown. She wandered through the apartment and helped herself to some juice from the icebox. There was no sign of Tom; he must have gone to work. She noticed a couple of photographs pinned to the noticeboard on the kitchen wall, amongst the newspaper cuttings and bills. In one, Tom—a large man in his mid-forties, with long hair and a straggly beard—had his arms around a young woman; she looked towards the camera, but her eyes seemed vacant, looking beyond the photographer into some unknown distance. The other was a slightly blurred likeness of a white-bearded, swarthy-skinned man wearing a turban. Smiling, he revealed teeth that looked badly in need of repair. Millie remembered that her sister had explicitly told her not to ask about a certain photograph Tom kept of an Asian man, under any circumstances at all. Millie was curious, but not curious enough to ignore Dorothy's advice.

She recalled having been woken early in the morning by what had sounded like a harmonium, but unless she'd actually dreamt the vaguely hymn-like music, she must have fallen asleep again after only a brief time, for her memory of it was slight and indistinct.

Given that Dorothy mainly had musicians for friends, Millie thought it likely Tom would turn out to be a musician of some sort. On the other hand, it seemed odd that a jazz trombonist like Dorothy would know someone who played hymns on a harmonium.

Millie went back to the bedroom and took a letter out of her case. The letter—which was from Dorothy— was creased with much handling, but she read it again. Dorothy's friend, Benno, had disappeared. He'd been working with her on a couple of investigations she'd taken on, in the role of amateur detective—the murder of the artist, Geoffrey Johnston, and the disappearance of Pamela Cotman. The last time Dorothy had seen Benno, he'd seemed excited about something, but he hadn't wanted to talk about it. He'd bought a ticket for L.A. and had called in on the way to the airport to say goodbye. That had been months back, and Dorothy had heard nothing from him since. Millie was in the States for the bodybuilding finals in Las Vegas, and Dorothy had asked her to try to find out what had happened to him. Dorothy suggested that Millie look up her old friend Tom Jackson in Santa Monica, as Benno had mentioned something about going there. The result was that Millie had been invited to stay in Tom's apartment for as long as she wanted.

2.

Millie backed the car out of the drive and started down Ocean Avenue past the rundown motels, corner groceries and cheap bars. She was suddenly struck by the difficulty of knowing even where to *start* to look for Benno. She pulled into the parking lot at the foot of the pier. A steep stairway led from the sand to the pier itself. She walked along the pier past the arcades, the fish-restaurants, the bait-stores. There was nothing here to connect with what she knew of Benno. At the end of the pier, there was a sign that pointed down a stairway to a lower level restaurant. The sign read: THE BENNY GOODMAN ROOMS. It was too much to expect anything from this, but Millie decided to try it anyway. She went down the stairs and slid onto a tall stool next to the counter.

—Hi, honey. What'll it be?

—Just black coffee and a couple of eggs, said Millie. The woman turned and called out the order to a thin man who stood at the grill a few feet behind her.

—Haven't seen you around here before, have I?

—No, I just arrived. I'm looking for this little guy I know, a clarinet-player, with a hunchback.

—Hey, Bill, she shouted. Come on down here. This girl's looking for Benno.

A man at the far end of the counter slowly turned and got up from his stool, and came down the restaurant towards her.

3.

Benno had been in the habit of lunching at The Benny Goodman Rooms most days, having discovered the place shortly after his arrival. But he'd stopped, more than two months ago, and the staff and regulars had assumed he'd left town.

—You know, I thought it strange the little guy didn't say goodbye, said Bill in a slow and thoughtful voice, leaning his elbows on the counter. We'd gotten friendly, me and Benno—sometimes, you know, we'd go back to my place and do a bit of jamming together....

He suddenly produced a Polaroid from his shirt-pocket and handed it to Millie. It showed Bill—with a large grin on his face—seated at an upright piano.

—Yeah, we had some good times, Bill said. I sure hope you find Benno, sister; and let me buy you another coffee, 'cause of you being Benno's friend.

Millie was a little irritated at being taken for a friend of Benno's—she had never really liked him, and was only looking for the missing clarinettist as a favour to her sister; but she let it slide. She asked Bill if she could have a tomato juice instead.

Having explained that she wanted to think things over by herself, she took her drink to a corner-table, and sat back with her eyes closed, hoping that some new idea might occur to her. She sat there for fifteen minutes or so, and would have left the place except for something that suddenly penetrated her consciousness from the other end of the room.

—*What?!*—she heard; an explosive sound that, as she found when she opened her eyes and looked over in curiosity, had apparently emanated from an elderly man with a bushy moustache who seemed oddly familiar. Then she remembered the photograph Dorothy had brought back from Boulogne. It was supposed to have been a group picture of Georges Gorin, Laura Jameson and Benno, sitting at a table together; but the image only showed Gorin at all clearly, with Benno's hand visible on one side and Laura's shoulder on the other.

Millie got to her feet and walked towards Gorin, who was talking with Bill. Gorin was saying:

—I suppose you like Bud Powell's playing, don't you? *Poor* Bud Powell. Terribly sad case, *what?!* I knew him, of course, in Paris –

—Aren't you Georges Gorin? said Millie, interrupting the legendary French novelist and raconteur. Gorin turned to face her, his mouth hanging open in surprise. He adjusted his glasses and gave her a long look, as if trying hard to place her.

—I'm Millie Evans—Dorothy's sister, she said, and Gorin's face broke into a smile.—Ah, he said, Dorothy Evans—*charming* girl. Shame about her friend Benno, though, isn't it? *Poor* Benno Lieberman—*such* a pity he's got himself lost. *What?!*

—I've been telling Mr. Gorin about old Benno having disappeared, explained Bill. Mr. Gorin being a friend of Benno's, you know.

—Did you see Benno while he was here in Los Angeles? Millie asked Georges Gorin.

—We met a couple of times in this very place, said Gorin. Of course, poor Benno was disappointed at having failed so dismally at trying to find Patty Waters. *What?!*

—But that was years ago, said Millie, who knew the story of Benno's attempts to locate the singer Patty Waters in New York.

—He tried again, though, said Gorin. But let's talk about Benno over dinner this evening—if you're free. I have to give an interview now—my new novel's just been published, *what?!*

Millie and Georges Gorin made an arrangement to meet later at a restaurant specified by Gorin, and the French writer left for his interview.

4.

Millie had spent the afternoon in looking around the city on foot. There'd been an unpleasant incident at one point: a man had suddenly stepped out in front of her as she was walking along; he was obviously intent on some sort of attack on her, and Millie had struck him across the throat with a karate-blow, sending him sprawling to the pavement. Not wishing to be detained, and possibly involved with the police, she'd hurried off before any onlookers had a chance to gather around.

Eventually, she discovered a gym that met with her approval, and occupied herself with a fairly thorough work-out. She'd intended walking to the restaurant, but she lost track of the time and had to take a cab to avoid being late.

Millie fell into a conversation with the driver about traffic jams in the city.—This morning, she told him, I was in my car, waiting for the traffic to move again, and I looked across to this other car and saw the driver shaving himself.

—Lady, said the taxi-driver, that ain't nothin': just yesterday, I saw this little guy with a hunchback, sittin' in his car—he was playin' this *clarinet*. Sounded just like Artie Shaw, that little guy did.

Millie had little doubt from what the cabby had said that Benno was still in Los Angeles. She questioned him further about the clarinettist's appearance, and everything he said fitted Benno. The puzzling thing was that he said Benno sounded like Artie Shaw. Benno's playing was more "contemporary" in approach; and the only Artie Shaw recordings he owned to liking wholeheartedly—she knew this from a talk she once had with him—were some of the Gramercy Five numbers from the early 1950s. She thought that perhaps for the cabby "Artie Shaw" was simply synonymous—in some vague way—with jazz clarinet playing. But when he said that Benno had been playing Shaw's Swing-period composition, 'Nightmare', her supposition was destroyed: the man did know his Artie Shaw; and just as obviously, Benno's musical concerns had mysteriously changed since he'd left London.

Millie thought of one last question.—Did he look as if he was happy? she asked.

—Lady, said the taxi-driver, that was somethin' you couldn't help but notice: that little guy had the saddest look on his kisser I've ever seen.

5.

If, on finding the restaurant, Millie was relieved to discover it to be an unpretentious place specialising in traditional Italian cooking, she was anything but pleased by her first sight that evening of Georges Gorin, who was already seated at a table towards the rear. He was wearing a white shirt with a design of small yellow flowers on it, and when he stood up to welcome her, she saw that he also had on bright green trousers—the brightest green she'd ever looked upon.

Georges Gorin had recently been to see Syberberg's *Parsifal* while he was in Paris, and he asked Millie if she'd had a chance to see the film yet, adding that it was currently being shown in Los Angeles. When Millie admitted that she only went to the cinema to watch thrillers, Gorin's mouth dropped open in amazement and, no doubt, disappointment.

—But it's a very erotic film, said Gorin. I feel sure you're someone who's interested in beauty. Therefore, you must be interested in eroticism. *What?!*

Millie put down her fork and spoon for emphasis, and said: Georges, I can be interested in beauty, surely, without there being anything erotic involved.

—I'd have to disagree, said Gorin.

—I can look at a flower and see that it's beautiful, said Millie. Where does eroticism come in there?

—The flower can have erotic associations that are related to its beauty, said Gorin.

—But when I see a flower, I don't *first* think of it as erotic, said Millie. If I associated it with something erotic, that would be secondary. What do you say?

—Granted, said Gorin.

—And there might only be this primary feeling for its beauty, continued Millie. From admiring the beauty of the flower, I don't have to go on to any erotic associations. Do you agree?

—I was thinking more of human beauty, said Gorin. When you admire a person's beauty, you also admire them sexually.

—If I have a friend whose face I consider beautiful, said Millie, or if I look at a very old person or a very young person and find them beautiful, there's again a primary feeling, and in any of those cases it would be unusual to go on to secondary erotic associations. Isn't that so, Georges?

—I have to admit, said Gorin, you're rather convincing.

—And in fact, isn't there this same separation between a primary feeling for beauty and a secondary association of the erotic in *all* cases? Unless you first see a person in erotic terms—and then their beauty is a component of your sexual feeling for them.

—Millie, said Gorin, I suspect you're a Platonist. Your sister described you as a level-headed, tough-talking body-builder with "muscle muscle"—*what?!*—but you're a philosopher in disguise.

—*Did* she? said Millie. By the way, she added, this spaghetti carbonara's very good. You obviously know your restaurants.

—Let me tell you a story, said Gorin. As you like thrillers, I'm sure you've heard of the novelist Cornell Woolrich.

Millie nodded.

—*Poor* Cornell Woolrich, said Gorin. *Such* a minor writer. Could never see why my friend Truffaut made such a fuss about him. I knew Woolrich, of course. When I was a very young man, living in New York. It would have been sometime in 1928—someone introduced me to him at a party. Cornell talked about his *mother* all the time—he was quite a bore, really. One day I met my friend Hart Crane in a bar, and he told me about a sailor he'd picked up the night before, who also talked incessantly about *his* mother. When he described the sailor to me, I realised that it had been poor old Cornell Woolrich, dressed up as a sailor. *What?!*

—Are you trying to tell me Cornell Woolrich was a *pansy*? asked Millie, putting her fork and spoon down again. The man who wrote *Phantom Lady* and *Night Has a Thousand Eyes*?

Gorin's face turned a deeper red. It suddenly entered his mind that Millie Evans might turn out to be a "queer-basher". He looked at her biceps and panicked.

—Excuse me just a minute, he said, getting unsteadily to his feet with the idea of making a quick exit.

—Hold on, said Millie. Sit down again, Georges. You haven't answered my question. You're *not* saying Cornell Woolrich—the man who wrote classics like *The Bride Wore Black* and *Rear Window*—was actually a homosexual? Or are you?

Gorin should perhaps have realised that Millie was teasing him, but didn't. She'd been slightly annoyed by Gorin's condescension towards Woolrich as a writer, and—knowing about his own sexual inclinations—she decided to discomfit him. In point of fact, she had no bias against gays.

—Oh, Crane didn't say the sailor was a *homosexual*, said Gorin. Good heavens! They just talked—about the sailor's mother. And it probably wasn't Woolrich at all—just someone who looked like him. Or else old Woolrich liked dressing up as a sailor for a joke—*what?!* You can't call a man a homosexual because he goes out at night dressed as a sailor.

—Glad to hear you say it, said Millie. By the way— we were supposed to be talking about Benno. He'd completely slipped my mind until just this minute.

—Benno! said Gorin, obviously relieved at the prospect of a different topic of conversation. *Poor* Benno Lieberman. I wish I could help you to find him.

—You said something about Patty Waters when I saw you at The Benny Goodman Rooms. I know that Benno was trying to locate her when he lived in New York a few years ago—in fact that was how he met my sister....

—Ah, but he'd found out she was in Los Angeles! That's why he came here.

Millie pushed back a lock of her auburn hair from her forehead. She said: How did he find out she was in Los Angeles?

—I told him, of course, said Gorin. *What?!* During a visit a few months ago, I happened to hear her sing in a small club. She wasn't using her real name, but I knew who she was. So I wrote to Benno, telling him about it.

She wasn't at the club any more when Benno got here—
and I've no idea if he finally managed to find her or
not before he disappeared. Though, he added, knowing
poor Benno, I doubt that he did.

6.

Benno sat on the bed in his room and stared at the dirty, peeling wallpaper.

How many more times? he thought; but he knew he had to do it. He put the recording of 'Carioca' on his battered-looking old record player again, and concentrated on the clarinet part. When the record was over, he shut the machine off and picked up his clarinet.

He found the final *glissando* difficult to reproduce— but then he'd always had trouble with *glissandi*. The rhythm was also uncongenial; Latin American rhythms were inextricably connected in his mind with Nestor Amaral and Xavier Cugat—despite the actual difference between confectionery of that sort and the vibrancy of Shaw's music.

Benno put down his clarinet. He had to admit he still hadn't got it right.

7.

When Millie returned from her dinner with Georges Gorin, she found Tom at supper, eating a plate of brown rice and vegetables, with boiled seaweed on the side. Tom explained that he'd arrived home late because of having to visit a friend in hospital. He'd heard from mutual acquaintances that the man had been attacked while out on a walk earlier in the day, and Tom went straight over to the hospital to see him after finishing work.

—Wow, he said (he always prefixed a statement that he considered revelatory with the word Wow), this friend of mine—Jim—was just walking along, you know, not doing anything wrong, because Jim's a good sort of cat, and this woman—who must have been some sort of *psychopath*, Millie—just up and chopped him across the throat, you know, with her hand—and poor old Jim goes smack down on the pavement and hits his head.... That woman must have been an *animal*, Millie; they shouldn't let creatures like that loose on the street.... You should watch out, Millie, there are a lot of cats in this town who don't have any higher awareness *at all*—they're mean, dangerous cats—like that psycho who attacked Jim today....

To change the subject, Millie asked him if he had any Artie Shaw records (she knew from Dorothy that Tom had a large collection of jazz recordings). Tom obligingly searched around, and came up with a handful of 78s, a 10-inch LP of the second Gramercy Five group and a 12-inch double LP of selected "hits". Tom went to his room to meditate, while Millie listened to the records. She was especially interested in the piece called 'Nightmare' that the taxi-driver had mentioned to her. Millie found herself immediately fascinated, and at the same time a little repelled, by the slow, pounding rhythm, the brooding chant-like insistence of the reeds and—swirling over the reed section—the lone voice of Shaw's clarinet. The claustrophobic, at times almost hysterical, mood of the piece—if certainly appropriate to its title—struck her as odd, being out of keeping with what she thought of as the optimistic, buoyant nature of Swing.

Millie shut off the stereo and tried to think out how this music might relate to Benno. Even if she allowed that Benno's concern with a rather contemplative form of modern jazz might reflect Dorothy's approach more than his own, she still could not imagine him being interested in this sort of music. Whenever you got an idea of Benno's own inclinations, you saw that he was actually less conservative than Dorothy. He'd experimented with free jazz in the '60s, and you couldn't imagine Dorothy having done that. More recently, he'd taken to listening to the composer and singer Meredith Monk; he even bought himself a Meredith Monk T-shirt. (When Benno wore his T-shirt to a party at Dorothy's, Dorothy met him with the exclamation: God, Benno, she looks just like Laura Jameson!)

If the mood of 'Nightmare' was to be taken as an indication of Benno's state of mind—and from what the cabby had said, this was entirely possible — then things had not gone well for Benno since he'd left London.

She thought about why she'd never liked Benno. She considered his clarinet playing to be lousy, although she knew this was scarcely a reason for disliking someone. Mostly, she decided, it was a matter of the way he was always hanging around her sister, as if he didn't have a home to go to.

Millie sighed. She was getting nowhere. She began to feel irritated at having to spend her time this way. Instead of searching for a missing clarinettist, she could have been lounging around Muscle Beach, displaying her muscle definition while getting a tan. But whatever she might think of Benno, he was her sister's friend, and if he was in trouble she felt she should help him if possible.

Millie sighed again. What would she do tomorrow? There were no leads to follow up—apart from trying to locate Patty Waters, in case Benno *had* been in touch with her, or checking if Benno was working with a band in any of the jazz clubs in town. Neither idea seemed very promising. Millie went to the kitchen to get herself a glass of milk, and then she went to bed.

8.

Millie had been woken in the night by a powerful beam of light flooding the room, accompanied by a loud whirring noise. The first thought that came to her was that she was about to be abducted by the inhabitants of a flying-saucer—but then she realised that it was the search-light from a police helicopter making a routine check, and felt annoyed with herself for jumping to such a fantastic conclusion.

After a leisurely breakfast, she went out for a morning run, hoping that the early exercise might prompt some thought of how to proceed with her investigation.

But the running didn't work as a stimulus. In fact after half an hour Millie decided to call it quits for the morning and go back to the apartment for a while. She stopped off for a coffee, and then took a short cut home—walking now, as somehow she'd lost the heart for running. At one point on the way back she passed a woman polishing her car; the woman called out to her, Hi, have a nice day.—You, too, honey, said Millie with a friendly wave, but the woman had already turned away. Shit, thought Millie; what *is* it with some people?

Back at Tom's, she read a David Goodis novel, *Down There*, which she'd picked up at a second-hand bookstall the day before. She knew the story-line of it from Truffaut's film, *Shoot the Pianist*.

Millie helped herself to some lunch, and then made coffee. She was wondering again what she should do next, when the telephone rang.

It was Georges Gorin, and he sounded excited.

—I know where *poor* Benno Lieberman is, Gorin announced. He's been put in jail. *What?!*

Gorin explained that he'd been watching TV late the previous night, and during a news broadcast he'd seen a brief clip of a familiar-looking hunchbacked man clutching a clarinet-case. Benno—for it was indeed he—had a manic expression on his face, and was being led away, in handcuffs, towards a police van. The news commentator briefly outlined the story: a brawl had broken out in a certain night-club when the clarinet-player in the house-band had run amok, trying to smash everything in sight and hurling chairs at anyone who attempted to stop him.

—I've been trying to phone you all morning, said Georges Gorin. I suppose I should have tried last night, but it was really very late, and I thought it could probably wait until morning. I'll meet you at the police station, if you like, and we can arrange bail together.

Millie immediately agreed to Gorin's suggestion.

She had no idea of what sort of condition she'd find the unfortunate clarinettist in, nor was she sure how simple it would prove to bail him out. She was glad that she didn't have to face the situation alone.

9.

Held up by traffic, Millie arrived at the police station to find Gorin and a bemused-looking Benno waiting for her on the steps. Georges Gorin, with an efficiency that surprised Millie no less than his generosity, had already paid Benno's bail, and the clarinettist was now in his legal custody.

As they all drove back to Tom's apartment, Benno whispered to Georges Gorin, You told me we were "waiting for a friend"—you didn't tell me it was *Millie*. Benno had surmised a long time ago that Millie disapproved of him, and he found it hard to credit that such an unlikely pair as Gorin and Millie Evans had rescued him.

They arrived back at Tom's without any mishaps on the way. Millie made some coffee, and they sat together for several minutes in an uncomfortable silence. Benno held on to his clarinet-case with one hand, as if he were frightened it might be taken away from him.

Finally Gorin said: Benno, why did you try to wreck that night-club? You managed to do *quite* a bit of damage. *What?!*

Benno's face brightened instantly.—Wasn't it wonderful? he said, smiling with pride.

—But why did you do it, Benno? asked Millie. And where have you been all this time? What have you been doing? And *why* don't you put down that clarinet-case—we're not going to steal it from you.

The smile disappeared from Benno's face. He was being asked to talk about a terrible period of his life.

Millie tried to sound as gentle as possible.—We've all been concerned about you, she said. Dorothy most of all—she asked me to try to find you. She's really been very worried about you.

—OK, said Benno. I guess I can tell you and Georges. But could I have a drink first—some vodka, maybe?

Millie searched around in the kitchen and came up with some vitamin-fortified wine, which Benno said would do. (Millie abstained because of her training; Gorin because of the demands of a refined—if occasionally eccentric—sensibility.)

Benno sat back in his chair, shut his eyes, and began to tell his story.

10.

—I ended up playing with that crummy band because I was hurt and confused, Benno said; I didn't know what to do or where to go. Those guys helped me out; but they also used me, and I'm angry about that.

Georges Gorin suggested that Benno tell his story from the beginning, so that they would have a clear idea of how his troubles had developed.

Benno accordingly began the telling again—slowly, and with a certain difficulty. (Not only because of the nature of the events he had to relate, but also because he was a reticent person who was unused to speaking about himself.)

He'd come to Los Angeles to find Patty Waters, as they already knew, and although he had eventually tracked down the woman Gorin had told him about, she was not the legendary vocalist. (—Forgive me, Georges, he said, but I don't think you could tell the difference between Patty Waters and Muddy Waters.) Nor did he have any luck with subsequent enquiries about the singer. This left him with the problem of going back to London and admitting his failure to Dorothy. So he kept putting off his return. But the more he lingered in Los Angeles, wandering the streets aimlessly, practising his clarinet in cheap hotel-rooms, and frequenting the Benny Goodman Rooms, the more he became convinced that he had failed in all the things he had set out to do in life. He had solved neither the mystery of Geoffrey Johnston's murder, nor that of Pamela Cotman's disappearance. As a musician, he knew that he was not in the first category of jazz players, unlike Dorothy. Finally, he had failed to win Dorothy's love. Even in choosing to remain with her as a friend, he was not sure he had done the right thing, for he felt that he could do nothing *for* Dorothy, in the sense of making himself needed.

Then one evening Benno returned to his hotel to find that his room had been broken into. Benno had brought few belongings to the States, and had acquired little since his arrival; but he did, of course, have his clarinet with him—and that, precisely, was what was missing. He had owned the instrument all the twenty years of his playing life—his father having bought it for him when he was thirteen. He was inconsolable.

He did, however, arrive at a plan for obtaining another clarinet. As he didn't have the money himself to buy one, he decided to ask for a loan from Suzanne Bishop, a woman he'd met at The Benny Goodman Rooms. She was a jazz enthusiast and an amateur pianist; she was also the owner of a small art gallery specialising in contemporary painting. Still in her early twenties, she was probably—Benno surmised—the youngest gallery-owner in Los Angeles. Benno took himself off to the Suzanne Bishop Gallery, where he found Suzanne engaged in a telephone conversation. He walked around the gallery, looking at the paintings while he waited. He stood in front of a painting with a monochrome background over which an evenly spaced row of vertical stripes of a similar hue had been painted, and over which, in turn, a succession of diagonal stripes in several different colours were arranged at varying intervals. Suzanne was saying over the phone, in her slightly haughty voice, *No*, I'm *sorry*, but I won't help you again, and that's final. Benno moved on to another painting—a completely monochromatic work of a particular black which would presumably have been achieved through painting thinly on top of an under-layer of dark blue. It didn't impress Benno. Suzanne was saying, I've *told* you, it's your problem, and I won't help you this time. Benno walked over to a third painting. It consisted of a rectangular blue expanse surrounded by a thin grey border. He glanced at Suzanne. A tall, handsome-looking woman, she was wearing an elegant black dress, gold bracelets and high-heeled pink shoes.

Her fox terrier, Leslie, was asleep near her feet.—Yes, I know you're in trouble, Suzanne was saying, but I simply won't do anything about it, and that's that; you'll just have to find someone else to help you. Benno left the gallery while she was still on the telephone.

There remained a certain fascination about Los Angeles for him. For instance, he was both amazed and delighted one day when he glimpsed one of his favourite actors, Robert De Niro, in a queue at a croissant shop. But small and superficial compensations such as this were scarcely enough to stem Benno's growing depression.

He began drinking heavily. This of course only complicated his mental condition; which was also made worse through an incident in the street one night. A man savagely kicked him in the leg for no discernible reason, shouting Freak! at him. After this, Benno's deformity worried him as it hadn't in years—he even showered in the dark to avoid catching sight of his body in the bathroom mirror.

From this point on, he began to develop what he later recognised as paranoid delusions. These fastened upon the character of Dorothy, who had, after all, rejected his love; and also upon his failure to solve the mysteries that he and Dorothy had investigated together. Benno had always wondered about the trombonist who'd disappeared from the *Blue Cross* jazz group, enabling Dorothy to make her professional début as his substitute. He began to suspect foul play, with Dorothy as the culprit. Once his mind had taken this turn, it continued relentlessly along the same wretched path. Dorothy had discovered Geoffrey's corpse—or so she had said. Couldn't she have murdered Johnston herself and then claimed to have innocently come upon his body? The more he thought about this, the more plausible it seemed to him. Dorothy had pretended to be investigating the murder in order to cover up her guilty secret, and Benno had unwittingly made himself an accomplice in this deception. The reason for killing Geoffrey Johnston seemed clear enough. Rose and Arturo, he persuaded himself, had hired Dorothy to do it. They claimed to have been Johnston's closest friends—but Benno felt he could see through this hypocrisy. He reasoned that Arturo had become resentful and embittered that Johnston, whose work he had championed over the years, had withdrawn from exhibiting his paintings, and finally ceased even to paint. Arturo had been made to look foolish by Johnston's actions. Rose, for her part, had undoubtedly been smarting all those years over Johnston's dismissive comments on her career as a video-artist. It all fell into place. So did the details of the next case: Pamela Cotman's disappearance. Benno had never trusted Pamela's boyfriend, Donald Wilson. Just to examine his record collection was enough to recognise what sort of shabby individual he was. (Imagine owning three records by Herb Alpert—a fact that Wilson had tried to cover up by claiming to possess only a single Alpert album—and *nothing at all* by Lee Konitz or Charlie Parker or John Coltrane.) Benno saw it this way: Wilson, having found out about Pamela's other boyfriend, had paid Dorothy to kill Pamela and get rid of her body. Then he had arranged to phone Dorothy about Pamela's disappearance at a time when Benno would be at Dorothy's place, to add plausibility to the mock-investigation they devised as a cover-up. Again he had been used, used! Lastly, there had been Laura Jameson. Benno felt indirectly responsible for Laura's fate. He knew that Laura and Dorothy had argued, and that the argument had developed from some remarks Laura had made about him. He would shake his head mournfully at the thought of this. There had been no need for Dorothy to have murdered Laura (for that was exactly what he assumed she had done)—and for his sake! He imagined that he would feel guilt for the rest of his days!

Such were the thoughts Benno had arrived at; and, he admitted, he was ashamed that he should ever have entertained ideas of this sort about Dorothy. Something of the desperate condition he had reached in time panicked him, and he sought help through a Church-funded counselling agency, where he had a number of sessions with a psychiatric social worker. One of the things this young woman did was to put Benno in touch with a bandleader of her acquaintance; Benno was offered a job in his band, with a new clarinet as the bait. Bait was, in fact, necessary, because of the nature of the band, which performed mechanically exact, note-for-note reproductions of old Artie Shaw performances, transcribed from records and tapes of radio broadcasts. As far as Benno was concerned, the result was totally without artistic credibility—Shaw's Swing performances were one thing, and Benno had an appreciation of their artistry, if not an actual liking for them, but lifeless replications of them forty years on were another matter. He took the job, just the same, as he wanted the clarinet; and he was also broke and unable to face looking for work himself. More than once the leader bawled him out for changing the notes in Shaw's solos.—From now on, the man had told him,

I'm the only one who says what goes. The rest is just bullshit. You got that, Benno? Benno got it, but didn't like it. In the end he went berserk and attempted to smash up the night-club that had come to symbolise his creative frustrations.—The rest, he concluded, you already know.

After Benno had finished his story, Millie and Gorin looked at each other with relief, for it was obvious to them both that however shaky he might seem, he had substantially recovered from the wretched condition he'd just described to them.

Tom arrived home, and Millie introduced Gorin and Benno to him. Benno was pleased to find out that Tom played the harmonium; he suggested that they might do some practising together. Then Benno suddenly said: By the way, Tom, who's the guy in that photo in the kitchen?—Wow, said Tom, glad you asked that, Benno....

11

After Tom had told Benno and the others about his guru, who was, Tom said, the One Living God, they all went out for a meal together to celebrate Benno's release. It was agreed that Benno would stay at Tom's place, at least until the time of his hearing.

A few days later, Benno was alone in the apartment, playing his clarinet, when he was surprised by a knock on the door. When he opened the door, he found to his amazement that Dorothy was standing there; she had a travelling bag and her trombone-case with her.— Benno! she said, kissing him on the cheek. Benno found it hard to recover himself from the shock of seeing her, but he managed to say, It's wonderful to see you, Dorothy, and helped her to bring in her things.

Benno was also surprised to see that Dorothy's blond hair had been cut quite short: formerly it had reached to her shoulders. (Occasionally she'd worn it in a ponytail.) But the change did nothing to detract from Dorothy's strikingly attractive face—with her fine-boned features and intelligent, hazel eyes.

She had brought a present for Benno: an elaborately framed print of Turner's *Rocky Bay with Figures*. She was talking with him about it when Millie came in. After the sisters had greeted each other, Benno showed Millie the print.

—Nice frame, she said, but I've never liked Turner much. Too grandiose for me. John Constable's much more my sort of painter.

—Millie, said her sister, that's the trouble with you— you don't like Turner. If you could learn to appreciate Turner, you'd get a lot more out of life.

—Yeah, maybe so, kid, said Millie, reverting to the *film noir* idiom she used habitually—and inexplicably— with Dorothy.

That evening Benno, Millie, Dorothy and Tom invited Georges Gorin over for a meal. While Tom and Millie were busy in the kitchen, Benno and Dorothy treated Gorin to a new arrangement Dorothy had made of the haunting Gordon Jenkins ballad, 'Goodbye'.

They took the piece at a slow tempo, and kept on the whole to a grave, formal elegance in their melodic interplay. Nevertheless, Dorothy had allowed both for the inherent beauty of Gordon Jenkins' melody, and for the opportunity of making short amelodic bursts of passionate lyrical playing on trombone at climactic points, over top of Benno's evenly placed clarinet notes.

Georges Gorin gave them an ovation, and Millie and Tom called out their appreciation from the kitchen.

For Guy Birchard and Anne Heeney, and to the memory of Pee Wee Russell

DARKNESS
ENFOLDING

Chapter One.

—No one even believes that we exist, Catherine said.

But Joseph knew that the statement was, strictly speaking, untrue.

He said: I've heard people mention your sect, just the same. And he asked: What are you, then?

—Blameless. Pure and undefiled.

•

Catherine was a library assistant at the university where Joseph studied.

Her face reminded him of a painting he'd seen in London's National Gallery, the *Portrait of a Girl* from Ghirlandaio's school, in which the beautiful modulations of line fulfilled an expression at once serious, yet tender and gentle. Her grey-green eyes held such quiet. It was this that gave her an aspect of sobriety. (As Joseph had cause to discover, concern would readily appear in these same eyes.) Shy, in some measure, she would initially lower her eyes when speaking to someone. If at times a spirit of ironic or sceptical humour revealed itself in her smile, there was evident warmth, too. Her small, slight figure; her fine-textured, chestnut-brown hair, which she wore in a ponytail; the grace of her slender neck—all these things Joseph found affecting. And her youth joined with them to quicken his affection.

Only her voice disappointed—to begin with, at least; for it was slightly high-pitched and thin.

Joseph had overheard her talking with a colleague, in a nearby café after work.—It must be your own unhappiness that draws you to unhappy people, her companion had said. If you were happy, you wouldn't want to see those people. She'd replied quietly yet distinctly: It's not like that.—What is it, then? he'd persisted.—It's because no one else seems to care, she said. But he still asked: Why should it matter to you? and amidst a sudden flurry of noise from a neighbouring table, Joseph caught only the word *bleeds* of her reply clearly.

●

—Have you been away? she asked him unexpectedly, when he brought his books to the counter. I haven't seen you for some time.

—I was in Dorset for three weeks, he said. My doctor's idea. I'm supposed to go away and rest every so often.

—Why? she asked. What's wrong?

—Arthritis, Joseph said; and he repeated: I just need to rest from time to time, that's all. He thought of some who'd assumed the term was for an illness that only afflicted the old, and had merely puzzled at it. But greater than the small worry this thought evoked, unease—submerged for some while—took hold of him, a combination of remembered pain and projected uncertainty. It showed itself in his face. Although she didn't reply, she continued to look at him; and from her gaze there was a flow of tender feeling, cancelling all distance.

The next time Joseph saw Catherine he asked her casually about herself: whether she liked the job at the library, and whether she thought she would stay in it for long. Then, having found his confidence, yet speaking too softly, he said: Would you like to have dinner with me sometime? She smiled, in her shy and appealing way, and said: Would I like to do what?—Would you like to have dinner with me?

And she said yes.

Joseph waved when he caught sight of her at the front entrance of the library. He walked up the steps, and stood facing her. It was a familiar situation: he had been thinking all week of what he would say, and now found himself without words.

She took the initiative by suggesting that they might go to a pizzeria she knew, and went on to explain that she was a vegetarian, which made choice of restaurants somewhat limited.

Flakes began to fall again, if barely (the ground was already covered in snow). But while they were still on their way to the pizzeria, the snow gained in density; they could only walk faster.

—Oh—*God!* said Catherine. The exclamation cut Joseph short, and he waited in silence for her to say something more.—I'm sorry, she said; but if you knew how I hate the snow!

—You *hate* it? he said. But why?

She appeared flustered—aware that her outburst had taken him aback.

—Well, she said, I suppose it makes me think of my childhood; I don't think I ever had winter

clothing that was warm enough when I was a kid....
I can remember standing around in the snow, during
recess, and shivering; and the misery I felt seemed to
me symptomatic—though I wouldn't have expressed it
like that then—of the unlovely and terrible world I was
forced to inhabit. I know it sounds melodramatic, but
when I see the snow I immediately think of how blood
would look soaking into it....

He felt strangely upset, if for no other reason than
his own delight in the snow—in laden boughs and,
against a pale sky, stacks, mounds of white.

Like the rain it was a power, additive in process and
effect; more so than the rain: for if the rain filled hollows
it also flooded off roofs and every convex surface; snow
settled and thus worked its change. Yes, he thought, it
worked a transformation; like the crazy old woman he
used to see in the street, writing Biblical proclamations
in chalk on the trees—so that the entire trunk was
eventually covered with white marks. Mornings when
he parted the curtains to reveal a white and unfamiliar
appearance where the familiar back garden should be,
always drew a feeling of wonderment. At a distance
the snow simplified everything, as in those black-and-
white photographs totally devoid of grey tones; but from
a closer position the forms of things were altered in

various ways, the snow making level, uniform surfaces here, and achieving beads, nodules, excrescences there, while leaves were slurred together like a brief passage of notes played *legato*.

He glanced ahead: in the middle distance stood a small group of trees, isolated. The clusters of boughs seemed lines etched into glass.

•

Seeking out topics, he began with the college and those who figured in its life.—But there's only one teacher who stands out, he said, and went on to explain his admiration for Maeve Robertshaw.

—I didn't learn anything important at school, Catherine said, and I didn't find university any better. My parents didn't teach me anything, either. My one real teacher helped me to change utterly. I was with her for a year, before she moved away—she spent her life continually wandering from one place to another.

—And what exactly did she teach you?

—That we have to escape from all the things that keep us imprisoned: history, nature, the body.... She taught me to recognise in myself a contradiction of those things.

—I'm not sure I understand, Joseph said.

But Catherine asked him to tell her about his illness.

He had been anxious, in fact, that he might not have done the right thing in mentioning it to her. That she wanted to know, he took as a favourable sign, and held back nothing from the account he gave.

Joseph described his condition as it had been until a short time ago: his fingers were badly swollen, and one finger refused to straighten; knees, ankles and feet also suffered from swelling; arm- and shoulder-joints caused him a great deal of pain, as did the wrists—pain that would make him yell out; while all through his frame he endured aches hour to hour, day and night. The most simple everyday things—rising from bed, and dressing; getting to his feet from a sitting position; walking; taking stairs—all these were to be accomplished only with absurd difficulty. At the same time there was extreme debilitation (compounded by lack of sleep) to be reckoned with. Gradually, over long months, the symptoms dwindled in severity, and were no longer disabling. There remained some inflammation in the joints, and he was easily fatigued; there was also the possibility, as he knew, of a relapse. He also knew how dependent he was on daily medication: there were signs of deterioration whenever he neglected the routine of his treatment. But on the whole he no longer looked ill; and he was as glad to be rid of this mark that singled him out for curiosity as he was for the physical relief.

Catherine had listened to his account without interrupting him by question or comment; now she said: I'm sorry that you've had to suffer like that.

They sat in silence for a moment. Then Catherine said:

—You know, don't you? No good and loving God created this world. It couldn't have been God—it had to be some nefarious and terrible power that brought it about. Why counter eternal good with evil, or everlasting joy with desolation? But that's what happened.

—Can't you see that? she asked.

She was smiling, and he was thankful that she was. At the same time he had no doubt that she was utterly serious. He couldn't frame an answer; he couldn't even bring himself to decide how much or how little he agreed with her.

•

Joseph walked with her to a small open park, a flat expanse of snow with trees and bushes; she lived on the other side of the park, she said, and there was no need for him to put himself to bother coming all the way with her.

—Joseph, she said, I have to be getting home—but come and see me at the library, and we can go somewhere for dinner again.

Catherine put her hands gently on his waist and kissed him on the cheek.

He watched her as she walked across the park, her figure becoming smaller, darker, more abstract; and harder to discern as she moved further from the light projected by the street-lamps that bounded its extent, towards the dark central area.

She turned around, waving her arms—no more in appearance than a gesticulating stick-figure now, pure sign.—Damn, she called out; it *is* freezing!

In the distance, someone was practising melodic phrases—simple, slow phrases—on a trumpet.

Chapter Two.

He woke from a dream about Xenia.

She and her family had rented, through some error, the same flat where Joseph and his parents were living; the two families were forced to live as equitably together as possible, until other arrangements could be made. Joseph was surprised to find that Xenia's family was distinctly rabble-like; their bad manners, noisiness and vulgarity contrasted with his parents' refined, genteel ways.

The waking reality was quite other than the dream: Xenia came from a polite middle-class background, whereas Joseph's family were self-educated working-class people—respectable, if unsophisticated.

She said: Don't pity yourself so much, Joseph.

He woke before he could answer her.

But he felt, and would have liked to have said to her, in the dream if not perhaps in any actual encounter, that it was despair that claimed him more times than self-pity: engulfing him, then letting him float adrift before overwhelming him again.

When someone permits their life to be a refuge for unhappiness, they invite rejection. Joseph knew this; yet he suffered when Xenia stopped seeing him. He had not concealed anything about himself from her eyes, anxious in their youthful uncertainty; and she'd accepted him, because she failed to understand what he told her. Xenia's generosity was shallow, though true— and soon eroded.

They'd met at a college party.

Joseph arrived alone. Maeve Robertshaw was already there, talking to a large-boned girl with jet-black hair cut very short, and a puzzled smile. Maeve said to the girl: Do you know the sort of thing academic philosophers churn out? You can't imagine how tiresome these people are. Nor how persistent! I'm in the position of having to keep up with at least some of their publications—and I can tell you, it's like wading through ordure.—Ordure, echoed the girl; isn't that rubbish?—No, replied Maeve, it's *shit*.

Maeve caught sight of Joseph and beckoned him over.—Joseph, she explained, I was just telling this young lady how *fascinating* academic philosophy is. Xenia, this is Joseph Dawe; he's one of my students, and *he* can tell you how wonderful it is to study philosophy while I go and locate some more wine.

There was, he noted, a nervous fluidity to Xenia's gaze; and in every aspect she seemed in fear of changing from a twenty-year-old, back into an awkward child. This quality, which might have irritated, immediately endeared her to Joseph.

He asked Xenia her subject area; and was bemused when she said it was animal bones.

—What are you studying? he asked. Veterinarian science?

—God no, she said, laughing. I'm an archaeologist.

Later, he was to see the basement room where she sorted through boxes of bones from excavations; while another student, working across from her, examined sheep's skulls. There was a large pile of flints in one corner of the room.

And she once, when they were walking together, picked up a dead sparrow from the pavement, carefully wrapped it in a handkerchief, then slipped it into her handbag.—I'll boil it down to see what the bones are like, she said.

●

Holding his hand, laying her head in his lap, or taking his arm during a walk—the habitual small expressions of Xenia's affection were what Joseph remembered above all.

But he also remembered—for there was no way to forget—their "differences".

He was envious of the younger men she knew. In his own eyes, the sheer dragging of the years showed, too clearly, in his features—there was a weariness offset only by a combative look that appeared in the eyes and through the set of the mouth. He would also compare himself unfavourably with many of her friends, because of the way they commanded space with their physical presence; his own body was slight and narrow-shouldered, yet lacking in any compensatory grace.

He was self-conscious from the first about the gap—nearly fifteen years—between their ages. At times it was only background: other things worked more damage in their relations; yet these depended upon the years in his life constituting the rift.

Joseph's father had been forced as a young man to leave his home-town; its industry was centred upon mines that were almost exhausted, and prospects of work were too dismal for him to remain. Sometime during Joseph's childhood, floods had struck the town; and on a television- screen he saw the heavy rains and rising waters obscuring like time the few discernible, nondescript features of buildings. This was, for Joseph, the image of the past—and he felt powerless to prevent each new day becoming integrated into this image. Small wonder, then, that Xenia appeared within his dreams to accuse him of self-pity.

If she clearly thought (though never explicitly said) that he was self-pitying, he thought she was naïve. He'd once been talking about his youth, when he was drafted into the Armed Forces during the time of the Vietnam War. Xenia asked what it had been like.—I never went, he said; my conscience told me I objected to the war.— What a pity you didn't go, she said, I'm sure it would have been really interesting.

He had lost hold at the end of that war, when the optimism of his generation dissipated itself. When he and his friends had been jailed, or attacked in the streets during demonstrations, they took it for granted that they knew and upheld some form of moral clarity.

(He still believed such clarity was possible; but he could find no firm location for it in any exterior faction, nor within the details of his own living.) He left the country of his birth. He decided to become a writer; and found he had too little talent. For a time, he drank heavily—but that didn't last, either.

•

Joseph and Xenia sat on the station platform, Joseph wearing both his own scarf and Xenia's, shivering with cold that he alone felt. When they reached his flat, he collapsed into bed, feverish; and upon waking the next day he was shocked to find how weak he was, and how painful it was to move his limbs. Over the next few months these attacks occurred at frequent intervals. When they ceased, the exhaustion continued, and so did the stiffness and pain.

He had fallen into a long illness. By the time that this became evident, Xenia had already left him.

Chapter Three.

—Joe, you always do that, Catherine said; you look at the sky (she meant the ceiling) or you look at your feet.

Then she said: I'd already invented your history for you. Of course, it wasn't *exactly* what you've told me....

She'd spoken of herself, too—telling him of the evening of her confirmation. The ceremony was held in a white-painted room, where she afterwards met, once every month, with others of her faith. She had sworn compassion for every being caught up in suffering. She had, at the same time, fore-sworn sexual relations. (And this—curiously, perhaps—didn't surprise or shock; Joseph only wondered achingly at how he could order his feelings to allow for its integration.

(A friend had once written to him, "Armstrong, 1929 and 'Some of those Days'. What was the tone they read in the blues? Of the loneliness which never knew words? Of the peculiar joy one senses in that loneliness (not happiness but the love which surpasses such—for only the lonely know what love is, that love cannot be found in the sweat glands, pores and hair)." Those words represented a particular horizon of feeling, the integrity of which he never doubted from the very first reading—however obscure the feeling appeared to him. In a similar way, he was drawn toward some process of integration; to simply reject his friend's words would have been inadmissible. Yet he couldn't decide whether this was because they called forth—awakened— something in himself, so strong it could not be refused; or because he wanted to disallow any intervention of distance between himself and his friend.)

He would have found it unbearable to doubt Catherine's sincerity, or her right to that sincerity.

•

While withholding his accord at certain points of belief, he felt sympathy for Catherine in all she said. It was as if a spirit of negation (to her eyes) preceded and informed existence. This demanded a further negation in response. He could admit the force in Catherine's belief that the human spirit only suffers in the body. That nothing spiritual shows itself in nature, was more difficult to accept. But Joseph admitted to himself that there were days when even a profusion of flowers appeared monstrous, a diseased condition. And it was true: harmony and splendour were mocked by disorder, suffering and horror. What surprised—impressed him, too—was that her convictions didn't bring her to despair.

•

Joseph's thoughts sometimes returned to what he had overheard of Catherine's conversation with the college librarian; and he wanted to ask, What about your friends?

But he never asked, and she didn't (for whatever reason) mention any friends.

In the same way, he didn't ask about her fellow believers, nor did she make more than the occasional passing reference to any of them.

She gave the impression of someone solitary.

•

Apart from the librarian at the college, Joseph had only once glimpsed a friend of hers, and that was by accident. He and Catherine were at dinner, in a Chinese restaurant close to her flat. A small group— Joseph recognised some as students from his college— occupied two tables at the back of the restaurant. They were playing charades, and Joseph called Catherine's attention to one young man—with handsome, intelligent features, and a flamboyant air—who was miming some unrecognizable action.—Oh, I know him! Catherine said, and went over to speak with him.

—That was Mickey, she said on her return. He was supposed to have been a keeper in a safari-park; he was feeding a giraffe, while shouting to visitors through a megaphone, to keep them away.

—Where do you know him from? Joseph asked.

But she merely said: Oh, he's just someone at the university, Joseph; and he was not mentioned again.

•

She seemed oddly drawn towards the 1930s and 1940s. The only time they went to the movies together, she'd insisted upon their seeing *Bringing Up Baby*—because, she said, she liked the idea of a comedy with Cary Grant, Katherine Hepburn and a leopard in the starring roles. She also admitted a fondness for *noir* films of the forties; and she had an *avid weakness* (as she put it herself) for their fictional counterparts: novels by writers as diverse as Chandler, Woolrich and Graham Greene.

Her small flat held few possessions. There was, however, a stereo; and she had a collection of jazz recordings that centred upon those same decades.

•

It was her Billie Holiday records that, more than anything else, they liked to listen to together.

Scarcely anyone believes the sentiments of the songs Billie Holiday sang—they're thought to be mere gilding for a more realistic love. Her singing (Joseph felt) was informed by the quality of her belief. The unhappiness of unrequited love absorbed into the greater pleasure of love itself, equally, the beloved's faults redeemed by the sheer fact of their being loved—this quixotic devotion to an ideal, so often involving a descent into degradation and unqualified hurt, can be an extremely moving quality in a person, perhaps especially when it's confused with warmth of feeling and sensuality.

•

Catherine asked Joseph if he knew an old ballad, called 'These Hours without You'.—Yes, of course, he said, it's a favourite of mine; and he sang it for her softly:

Can it be true that I wake
To these hours without you?
I sleep and dream a dream to share.

All the lonely day I don't dare
To even speak your name. For I love you:
I'd forsake the world for your sake.

They were listening to Billie Holiday singing 'Don't Explain', and suddenly, echoing the words that had just been sung:

—You're my joy, Catherine said.

—And pain? he said, completing the line.

—No, she said; no. She kissed his hand.

Held by her gaze, he was willing to believe that some unknown grace resided in him, obedient to her eyes.

The instinct of love for her leapt up; but where could it lead?

He thought of the room with the white walls, as she had described it for him: bare of all but a table draped with white linen, lit candles, and a bowl of water in which the faithful ritually washed their hands. To deny passion its indulgences, while cultivating compassion.... He could not imagine Catherine ever lacking in compassion. It suffused her glances; and it flecked her voice with warmth, making it seem more resonant than he had at first thought. But to bring forth compassion.... Was it because the needs of others, specific individuals with particular needs, provoked

some invisible fructification? Her joy.... *You're my joy.*
The phrase transfixed him.

He'd stayed, talking, until late; and it was raining:
so that Catherine suggested he sleep at her place and
return home the next morning.

Joseph washed in the bathroom while Catherine
improvised his bed from cushions and blankets. The
thought touched him that she might, after all, desire
intimacy; his better judgment dismissed the notion
almost as soon as it had appeared. He knocked on the
bedroom door and she called out for him to come in.
The room was in darkness, but he saw in the light from
the hallway, as he stood at the threshold, that she was
in bed, and that his makeshift bed had been arranged
at a short distance parallel to her own. He closed the
door and traversed the remembered space; pulled off
trousers, socks and shirt; and slid under the blankets.
He lay beneath the sloping sky-light, closed off by a
blind; the rain beat against the glass with a sound like
the crepitation of burning wood.

The obscurity was instinct with Catherine's presence,

because she had entered into it. His eyes sought and missed her lineaments the darkness absorbed. So that the dark was claimed as a second face: it was Catherine's face, yet it resisted perception. And it flashed into his mind that this face was surmounted by a crown of splendour, which was also part of the dark.

•

Maeve Robertshaw had said to Joseph: the divine was revealed through the human face. Catherine would probably have asked, sceptically, if a face could be perfect and wounded. For Catherine, the divine might have been symbolized by the upmost flames that dissociate themselves from the body of a fire, suspending themselves in air briefly before disappearing. Or a bird flying upwards, redeemed from the earth; perfect and whole.

Maeve had asked—or said—in one of her lectures: What is it in the human face that claims a further space—a space that is always beyond our wish and ability to comprehend it? How to say, as Levinas says, that this space is the ethical?

But Catherine told Joseph, You need to close your eyes when you stand before another person, if you really want to enter into their presence. Joseph repeated this to Maeve; she crinkled her nose in irritation, and lifted her elegant hands as if to wave the unwanted notion away.—Oh how *boring*! she said.

With his eyes open, yet in darkness, Joseph discovered what Catherine had meant.

Chapter Four.

He was standing in the college bar, when someone slapped him on the shoulder. He turned his head and saw that it was Catherine's friend, the young man who had been playing charades in the restaurant.

—Do you remember me? Mickey said. I'm sorry I didn't come over and introduce myself that evening—but I always suspect Catherine wants to protect other people from me.

—Yes, I remember you, said Joseph—but what do you mean? Are you serious?

—Well, half-serious, let's say. I'm sure that I'm decadent in her eyes!

Joseph wondered if he was supposed to feel embarrassed. He said: I'll buy you a drink, if you'll explain what you mean by saying that.

—God, said Mickey. Only *one* drink? But let's go somewhere else. I know a much better place than this....

•

Although Joseph had never been inside a gay bar before, it wasn't at all difficult for him to recognise, not merely a number of those very flamboyant gay men, with their obvious affectations of speech and gesture, but also several male prostitutes.

—Anywhere else in Europe, Mickey said, I could have taken you to a place where there'd be back rooms for doing all manner of things.

—What in particular? Joseph asked.

—Oh, *Joseph*, use your imagination!

Joseph thought it significant that Mickey chose to be apologetic: the bar indeed seemed an anticlimax. Catherine's regard for "blamelessness" (as she called it) was far removed from anything priggish. As if in reply to Joseph's thoughts, Mickey said:

—I don't want you to misunderstand; Catherine's always stopped short of any *open* disapproval of the way I live—and as you can see, I'm not *afraid* of anyone disapproving. It's those beliefs of hers that I mean! I was so shocked when she first told me about them, I kicked a couple of phone-boxes on the way home, to let off some emotion.

—You think she's intolerant? Joseph asked.

—Well, she doesn't act as if she were; and God knows, she's as kind as anyone I've ever met. It's her ideas—they're so strict and severe and bleak. And for heaven's sake, the girl doesn't believe in sex!

A tall woman with peroxide blond hair and heavy black mascara came over to their table to ask for a light. Joseph had noticed her when he first came into the bar—for she was the only woman there. She rejoined her companion, a pudgy man in a business suit. Joseph heard him say to her: We can go anywhere you like, I'll take you to the best restaurant in town.—She's a prostitute, isn't she? Joseph said to Mickey; not because she was uncertain of it, or because he felt Mickey needed to be told, but as an idle comment to fill a gap in the conversation. Mickey looked at him incredulously.— *He*, Joseph, not *she*; and he giggled at Joseph's naïvety.

—I'll tell you about an incident I once witnessed, Mickey said; it might give you a different insight into our friend Catherine. He raised a hand.—Oh, it's nothing that reflects badly on her; don't worry, it's not *that* sort of story!

He told Joseph that he and Catherine had dined together one evening; after their meal, Catherine suggested a walk. They were walking with no particular destination in mind, and eventually found themselves lost, wandering streets of which they lacked comprehension. But neither of them felt this a cause for concern. They sat down on a public bench, and she suggested they tried talking to passers-by and see what happened. It was beginning to get dark. As a man walked past, Catherine shyly smiled and said hello; the man either didn't hear or chose to ignore her.—Your turn, she said. This time a dog came by, and Mickey called to it. The dog came up to him, all curiosity and friendliness.—That's not exactly fair, she said; I meant *humans*.

—So much, said Mickey, for what I'll call the prelude to this story.

—We set off again, he continued; in time we found ourselves at a pub, and Catherine agreed to go in with me. I went to order at the bar, and who should I see? A really obnoxious guy from the college, named Johnny. Do you know the guy I mean? No? Well, you wouldn't want to. He once pointed out a girl that he had the hots for, and said: Wouldn't it be *really* exciting to cut her breasts off? I could see that he meant it, as well.

—He didn't spot me at the bar, and I returned to Catherine as quickly as possible. We talked for a while, and then I went to take a leak. When I got back, I saw that Johnny had seated himself at our table; he was holding forth to Catherine in a drunken, nasty fashion. He didn't even bother to acknowledge me, the creep, but just carried on as if I wasn't there. I felt like pissing in his lap—it made me regret I'd just been.—The more arbitrary your desires, he was saying, the better. I want to crap on conventions –

—That's not the point, said Catherine.

—*What*? he snapped at her.

—Conventions, she said. They're not the real issue –

—I can do anything, he broke in, that I wish to—rape, steal, murder, if I choose—and do you know why? Because there's nothing more sovereign than my will. Asserting my will to the utmost, I become God—the only God there is.

—Catherine turned to me, Mickey continued; she said, I thought you meant *humans*. Of course, I knew exactly what she was referring to, and I started giggling.

—What's funny? Johnny said. Are you going to let me in on the joke?

—You said you were God, Catherine said, but you're not even God's snot; that's the joke.

—So help me, Mickey said to Joseph. Well, I was in stitches; he was *so* angry. But I confess it shocked me, at the same time, to hear Catherine come out with such a thing. Johnny went off cursing us both, *rather* loudly; and Catherine touched my arm, and said:

—Nothing impure is worthy of the name of God.

—You were shocked, Joseph said, because she's always so gentle?

—Mmn, said Mickey. That's it.

—Later, he continued, we talked a little about Johnny, and I mentioned his comment about the girl's breasts. Of course, she was disgusted. But then she told me about Saint Agatha –

—She refused to sacrifice her virginity to a lecherous and powerful lord, said Joseph; he had her breasts cut off.

—Yes. And I began to say, Well, if you believed in what Catholicism taught—and that was as much as I managed to get out.—But the Church! Catherine said. I can tell you the story of a girl who refused to lose her virginity to a cleric—this happened in the twelfth century—and she was burned at the stake as a heretic.

●

—A small and unsteady light, Joseph said, wrested from utter abandonment.

He and Mickey watched as a Down syndrome girl—with joy in her eyes—ran down a passage of the underground, her companion calling after her in vain.

—Eurydice would run like that, Joseph said, past the multitudes that could be barely sensed along the dark corridors of the Underworld.

—What else have you got to drink? asked Mickey. Joseph had invited him back "for a nightcap"—and Mickey had quickly worked his way through whatever remained of bottles of whisky, gin and vodka.

—Why haven't you passed out by now? said Joseph in a mock-exasperated tone. I haven't anything else; you've cleaned me out.

—Let me tell you a story, Mickey said. A true story—about myself, what's more. I lived in Germany as a child—my father was stationed there with the British army. Somehow, I ended up in a children's choir that went around the hospitals at Christmas, singing carols to the patients. On one occasion, we sang 'Silent Night' outside a patient's room—I didn't know at the time why we didn't go inside to sing to him—and a nurse came out when we finished and told us that Herr Rudolf Hess had enjoyed our singing, and thanked us very much.

—It's a good anecdote, said Joseph. Any reason for telling it to me?

—Oh, I don't know. I suppose it's got *something* to do with innocence.

—Well, look, he continued. The boys I like are young enough to inspire an idea of innocence—and it's the idea I'm interested in. Sex and innocence make a beautiful combination. But the innocence is only a question of an image—a fleeting image, an elusive image, if you like.

—I need, he said, that contradiction of innocent beauty and sex. What else would allow me to escape....

—Escape? asked Joseph.

—From everything that's routine and banal—and Mickey waved his arms expansively, as if to show how prevalent the routine and the banal really were.

—But, he went on, what sort of places do you think I have to try and find innocence in? I've sometimes imagined being confronted by myself as I was when I was a kid. What would I say to myself? The child I was would be disgusted by the idea of my hanging around public toilets. And the clubs attract some dangerous characters. There've been a series of stranglings recently....

—Mickey, said Joseph, we'll have to continue this another time. I need to sleep now.

Joseph fetched blankets from the bedroom, and arranged them on the couch for his guest.

In the morning Joseph found that Mickey had left without waiting to say goodbye. A note had been placed on his desk:

> Dear Max,
> Thanks for the interesting night. So that's what they mean when they say "doing *it* to Webern". Crazy. You are a bit too rough, though. Be careful next time.
> See you around the lindens,
> Heinz.

It was an impudent joke, but it nevertheless amused Joseph. He laughed as he screwed the paper into a little ball.

Chapter Five.

—Tell me, Joseph said, about the woman who became your teacher.

—When I was a child, Catherine said, I thought I was like the other children I knew, and that I'd grow to be like the adults. I was taught I belonged to a society, a country and a history, because of accidents of time and place; and I was made to feel that I was part of nature —a physical organism amongst other organisms. I might have merged entirely with those dreams. But I was always uneasy about the way people expected me to be: my parents; my teachers; other children; and then later, my fellow students.

Catherine continued:

—She found me sitting in a cafeteria, having tea; she sat down opposite me and began to talk—and the things she said were exactly what I'd needed all my life to hear.

—Who, I thought, could she be? For I was marvelling at how much her words had affected me. She smiled, and said: I came here for one reason only: to talk to you.

—With her help, I left off being the person I thought I was; I began to retrieve myself from all the moments of my past in which I'd lost myself. It was like a building—

an invisible building; you go over it in all its details so thoroughly that you can then trace through it the real lines of your spirit.

—And she left you, Joseph said.

—Well, yes—Catherine looked directly at him— yes, she went away.

—But the letters, she said. She sent me letters that dazed me with her love.

•

Side by side on the wall were two large black-and-white photographs of Botticelli's *Abundance*. Shepherdess of children, who retires into her own resplendence. Plenitude animates the lithe, graceful figure as an air or ghost. One photograph reproduced the drawing as black and grey lines, with white highlights, on an off-white ground; the other, a negative print, reversed the black to white, the white to black.

Joseph sat opposite these panels; Maeve lounged on a couch beneath them, with her legs pulled up and her head tilted back. Joseph sipped at the cognac she had brought him. He said: I dreamt last night that I was walking in a desolate field of volcanic ash, and I came to a chair, standing by itself in that field. Then I heard a voice—someone singing—and in the distance I saw Catherine. There was a pathway of white stones, through the field of ash, and she was doing a soft-shoe routine on the stones while singing a song. I could only make out the words of one line: "It's got to be a moral story...."

He fell silent. Maeve said: Is that all?—Yes, said Joseph. He took a sip of his cognac.

Maeve drew the hair away from her brow in a sudden gesture with both hands; the unexpectedly bared forehead lengthened her face in a way that startled him.

—The thing I like about your dream, she said, is that Catherine was moved to dance.

—By the way, she continued, I once knew a Jesuit cardinal who was utterly *obsessed* with dancing. He was asked to appear in a television film about tap-dancing: it was the highpoint of his life.

Joseph had in fact lied: he'd withheld the last part of his dream.

He had tried to run to Catherine, but his legs were stiff with arthritis; he could only hobble, painfully. When he was no more than half way towards her, he suddenly found himself confronted by Catherine's colleague from the library.

—She's ruining herself, he said to Joseph. His voice was shrill, petulant.—She squanders herself on people who aren't worthy of her. I've watched her—I know! The man grabbed Joseph's arm.

—I don't want to hear this, Joseph said.

As Joseph shook himself free, the man blurted out:

—And then there was you! Don't worry—I followed the pair of you—more than once! I *know* what's been going on between you!

And that point Joseph had awoken.

•

When he left Maeve's, the sun was shining on a cherry-blossom tree at the front of her house. Each cluster of blossom was fused into a lucent ring or halo surrounding a darker centre.

Catherine would take no interest in such a sight, Joseph knew; the thought moved him. Neither blossom—nor eyes.... (Maeve, on the other hand, was particularly drawn to people's eyes. Portraits, for her, were always portraits of eyes.)

Oh Catherine, he thought, a line may lead from known threshold through unknown night. And there, in the night, visible beauty gives its place to invisible beauty.

She had his hand (he felt the touch, always). No matter, then, if the way was irrevocable, on which she took him to dwell in darkness.

AN ANGEL
IN THIS PLACE

Trees and bushes were like smoke as the train drove past—smoke penetrated by intermittent lights.

The palm of the hand was mute, pressed flat against the glass surface. The power of expression it had forfeited passed into the ring on her index finger, vibrant, lustrous.

John had dreamt of his friend Paul the night before. Dreamt of walking down a street in Athens, thinking that he might somehow find Paul, and then Paul was before him, dressed in an army uniform, smiling with pleasure at seeing him.

Looking into Fran's eyes, John lost himself in the depths of a darkness, from which he had no wish to emerge.

Holding her hand, now, he remembered the night they'd spent talking and drinking with her brother: how they had all stretched out on the floor of her room to sleep, the men on either side of her; under the bedclothes, he'd held her warm hand.

Two police officers stood questioning a man on the station-platform near where they alighted. There were more policemen gathered further down the platform; and as Fran and John walked towards them, John noticed flecks of blood on the ground. When they reached the place where the second group was standing, he saw a bright pool of blood, and a body slumped on a seat.—Oh, Jesus, he said; and Fran tightened her hold on his arm as they walked on.

They stopped for a moment along the way.—Let's have another drink, he said, but she declined. He took a long swallow, finishing the bottle of wine originally intended for the party. The night seemed to have been hammered across its entire extent, like a sheet of copper.

—We're friends of Jacob's, he said to the young woman who answered the door. They went into the front room, and John found his way to the wine table. He couldn't see Jacob anywhere amongst the various groups.

Nicole, dressed as always in black, stood in a corner, holding a chrysanthemum in one hand, a cigarette in the other; her hair as yellow almost as the flower. Tall and attractive, she drew interest from all around the room; while seemingly remote from that interest.

He'd seen her twice before. Once, he'd met her and Jacob at a cinema, for a screening of Val Lewton's *The Seventh Victim*. She'd carried a long, stout black cane topped with silver; and however theatrical her appearance, her aloofness intrigued him.

The other time, he'd recognised her in a café, but without being noticed in turn. She'd sauntered from one end of the counter to the other and back again, finally ordering a meat samosa which she ate standing at the cash register.

They found Jacob in the kitchen, where he was trying to persuade a pretty, blond-haired teenager to kiss him. The boy looked abashed when Fran and John entered the room, but Jacob was amused.—John! he said. Do you remember the Rothko room?—Of course, said John. I caught you trying your charms on some innocent, in front of the very paintings I'd come to see that day.—You were shocked, said Jacob.—Only because they were Mark Rothko's paintings, John replied. They're paintings for contemplation, and that was what I was there to do—contemplate them.—How reverent! said Jacob.

Glass containers and pieces of fruit stood on a red-painted shelf against the red wall. Jacob leaned against a cupboard, on the door of which postcards had been tacked: a Balthus painting of a naked girl in an erotic posture; a Renaissance picture of the martyrdom of St. Sebastian; and finally, a photograph of a group of Minoan clay figures, a lyre-player with three dancers.—Paul? John asked.—Oh, said Jacob, the dancers! Paul sent the postcard a couple of weeks ago.—What did he have to say?—That he's in the Greek army, which we knew, and that he hates it, which we knew. What do you expect him to say?

—You know, said Jacob, when I first met Paul I thought he was a psychotic.

Fran said: That's unkind of you, Jacob.

—Oh, said Jacob, you must understand how I felt: the disconnected sentences, the sudden fits of laughter.... He stopped, seeing John staring at him.—Mind you, he said, I thought *John* was a drug-addict when we first met. You know: the pale complexion, the haunted look in the eyes.

—But Paul, he continued, was simply an exception, and he was wonderful. I took him to a gay bar once, for a drink; I slipped out to get some cigarettes, and when I entered the room again and saw him there, I couldn't help drawing a contrast between him and all the others. It wasn't just that he was the only heterosexual in the room. Everyone there was there to be seen, and worse than that, they looked exactly as they were supposed to look; Paul was free of those things, and I respected him for it. I went up to him and said, You look like an angel in this place.

Fran and John left the house to take a walk in the night air.

On the way back, he began vomiting. He leaned against a wall, and saw with dismay the thin stream emerge from his mouth, again and again.

Fran sat on the edge of the bed, watching him. He wanted to sleep, but the noise of the party was too loud.—You remember the blackbird? he asked. She didn't reply.—That night we walked along the South Bank, and listened to the blackbird singing on top of one of the buildings, he said.—Yes, I remember; but you should try to sleep. She stood away from the bed.—I'll come back in a little while, she said.

He'd told her the bird was singing for her, out of love; and she had called out to it: Here I am, my darling!

The room trembled, like the tilt of a roof intersected by a bird's flight; as the memory shook open his feeling for her.

He was walking along a road, and he saw Nicole coming towards him. Nicole said, Why don't you try not to drink so much?—Why do you have a pentagram in your room? he asked.—It's something different, she replied, and shrugged her shoulders. John said: Someone once wrote that God's freedom was such that He could utterly annihilate a person without other reason than His will to do so. He also wrote that no necessity made God become man; He could have become an ass, or a stone in the street.

But he was sitting at a café table, with Paul beside him, and Paul was laughing hysterically.—What does the stone say about that? he asked, and began laughing again.

—Well, you've really come! Paul had said, when they'd arrived at his cottage in Meligalas Messenias. And: She has *lovely* dark brown eyes! You didn't tell me that, he'd said of Fran. Paul had brought out a large jug of ouzo; Fran drank sparingly, but John tried to match Paul's prodigious capacity, with the result that he spent the later part of the evening lying down in the next room, from where he could hear Fran and Paul talking and laughing.

Fran had taken a photograph of Paul and John standing on a street corner in Meligalas: Paul large and nervously awkward, looking at the camera with a somewhat bemused expression; John small and fragile by comparison, and wrapped in a trench-coat.

They'd sat in the kitchen of the cottage, or in cafés, or taken walks along the earthen roads lined with large clusters of cacti, and Paul had spoken with bitterness and hatred of everything that he understood by the word *history*: exterior temporality that dominated the individual.—The kingdom of evil, he said. I want it to end! History: what a shitty idol to have! It's all control and power, from beginning to end. For me, the end's come; and none too soon!

John had felt that he was being ironic, for he'd already been called up for the army, and had only a couple of months of freedom remaining to him. But he'd said, What end, Paul? How has it ended? Paul had responded with uncomfortably loud laughter, before he'd answered: *Wood and stones are my masters, they teach me what teachers cannot say.*

Fran came back into the room and sat down on the bed again; she said: I thought I'd see if you were any better.—What have you been doing? he asked.—I've been chatting to a few people, she said, but I'm not sure I really like it here.—I dreamt about Paul, he said.

Walking along the road that led to the station, neither of them felt like talking. It had been this road he had dreamt about; where he'd seen Nicole, before the dream had shifted to the café with Paul.

John remembered an evening when he and Fran had lost their way looking for a friend's house; coming to a street corner, they'd gazed together at the fallen petals at the far end of the street: pools of sugar spilt on the dark pavement.

LADY GAY

With Philip this afternoon—we met and had lunch, and there were two others. One, a man, was involved in what he termed "visionary architecture". He showed us some models of his designs, with corresponding drawings. I detested them. And I could see that Philip was, at least, bored: he kept trying to change the subject. (He talked about the gangster Dutch Schultz.) The architect, an Italian, wouldn't be swerved from his purpose. His drawings and his models were brutal-looking, and didn't appear in the least functional. I couldn't see in what way they were "visionary", either. Philip was now saying something about the crime-inducing effects of certain environments. At that point we realised we'd been given cheese sandwiches instead of chicken. We both glared in the direction of the waiter. The other, a young woman, showed us in turn some photographs and drawings plotting the windfall of an orchard. The drawings were precise yet witty; they showed a real feeling for plasticity and formal structure. It must be love. We ordered coffee; except for Phil, who ordered tea. You can live in an orchard. Not for too long at a time, of course—you need shelter, for one thing. You could live in the tracing of that windfall. But you could not live in those "visionary" buildings; nor would you desire to. Philip and I said goodbye to the Italian and the young woman artist, and headed for a subway. We picked up a magazine and looked through the list of art exhibitions.—That'll be thirty pence, the news vendor, a fat young woman, said in a cold voice. We put the magazine down and, having taken note of two exhibitions, headed off. You loved me.

(*Lady Gay*—1.) Mansions. Smell of incense. Clarified butter. Water in a pond. Water in a well. Water I would not drink—the look and the odour. These were the mansions, a darkness in many rooms, a dank odour; other rooms were opened by a strong, piercing light. Light from the snow. I had had trouble reading the numbers, but—now we were here.

—*What do they want from me?* she screamed, tearing the air which beseeched her. The rooms were full of ghosts. They stood in rows, like refractions of light, they stood demanding—*I want, I want*—catching at the sleeves; paupers.

She fed the children: Lucy, who was five, Sam, who was seven, and Joanna, eight. Would never have enough—always wanting more. And *why* did Sam throw his on the floor like that?

Love before the fire. The nights cold. And the house: cold. It was some time before—it is always some time before, and you know by the numbers: you count. And if you count forwards? She said, My best friend—. She'd lost count. She said, My best friend was in South-East Asia, and had been planning on continuing on to England; she contracted typhoid, and died. I'd cared very much, she said, water in her eyes. But it was another story, another death....

1974 (winter): I was being kicked out of a house I'd lived in for the past two years, and I was also without work. A friend suggested I phone the Russian poet Joseph Brodsky, who was staying in London at the flat of a mutual friend, G., in her absence, and explain my problem, adding that if G. had been there she'd have let me move in. (This being in fact sheer presumption.) *I can visit, once more,/ this abode of pure love....* I decided, in desperation, to make the call to Brodsky; he reluctantly agreed that I should move in. Another friend helped me to get my belongings together, and we drove in his car to the flat. Brodsky let us in; he seemed more dubious, but said we could bring up my belongings. *Between the two, though, there exists a thread,/ which we can call, quite simply, an apartment.* We'd carted most of the stuff up the three flights of stairs when Brodsky's English friends, who had rented the flat from G. on his behalf, turned up and demanded that I leave. They explained that Brodsky needed peace and quiet in which to write. The celebrated poet wore the same pained expression he'd worn since he answered the door to us. No goodbyes. *And now, like a path to a gateway,/ he leads me out into the dark.*

(*Lady Gay*—2.) She asked them, Why have you come to my house? They shook the snow off their clothes.—Step aside, ma; we're coming in. This was after their deaths.

Through the window of the bathroom (the window open) bright, clear sunlight: in imagination, a sea out the window, blue; in fantasy, nothing but the same light of fact.

(*Lady Gay*—3.) It was the day they'd be departing. Lucy, Sam, Joanna. She'd made sure they'd packed their things and that all else was in order. Habitual. The children were to go—Well, I *hate* boarding-school, I *hate* teachers, I *hate* ALL that stuff. Splat, someone's meal had landed on the floor, behind her. She turned around. The house gradually dissolved.

Today, walking in Camden Town, I happened upon a woman I know slightly who writes poetry. We briefly exchanged hellos. Last time I was at her home some of her book-shelves fell on top of a Persian poet. Maybe I'll visit her place sometime again. Continuing up the road I eventually reached where I'd been aiming for.

(*Lady Gay*—4.) It was lonely without the children in the house. She didn't even keep any animals. Neighbors? What? Bachelard writes, *those black holes which interrupt the line of recounted dreams are perhaps the mark of the death instinct which is working at the bottom of our shadows.* Do I believe this? No. Did she believe it? Yes.

(Mid-1972): I had answered an advertisement for a room, which I would have had to share with another occupant, an ex-art student named Frank. I went over to the place, in Chelsea, and met Frank, who turned out to be a pleasant and amiable young man. There was some mix-up over arrangements, and I ended up in a rapidly decaying Buddhist community in Clapham instead. Finding myself fed up, I dropped Frank a line and asked if he still needed someone to share his place. I then received a phone-call from a young woman who lived in the house Frank had been in, to tell me he'd suicided. She said, Do you still need somewhere to live—you said the place you were staying in was like a shrine-room.—Not *like* a shrine-room, I replied; *is* a shrine-room.

(*Lady Gay*—5.) It had been about two months that the children had been gone. (Winter.) There was knocking at the door; she went to open it, and there were her three children: Lucy, Sam and Joanna. They were not supposed to be home. She decided to leave those sort of questions until later.—Are you hungry? she asked, looking from face to face.

I had met an English sculptor who lived in Paris but had come to London to try to arrange an exhibition. We went to see a large exhibition of contemporary sculpture together. He'd been bemoaning the gallery set-up, where "intimate contact" often *did* seem the key, like the story goes. We were both rather bored by the exhibition. My sculptor acquaintance spent most of the time picking conversations with various people, and swapping addresses with them.—Never know when this sort of thing will come in handy, he said to me. After a while I noticed an American painter I knew; he was with some other guy, and travelling fast.—See you later, he said as they rushed past me. There never *is* any later.

(*Lady Gay*—6.) (Cancelled.)

I was at the library, crouching down at some shelves in the Religion section. A neat, well-dressed young man bent down in my direction and asked if I was interested in religion. I said I was looking for something on Gnosticism.—Are you interested in religion? he asked again.—No, I lied. He smiled and left.

(*Lady Gay*—7.)—We don't want any of your food nor your drink, mother. Their faces seemed very pale. Unsmiling.—*Well,* if you've *already* eaten, that's OK, kids. They shook their heads. She never understood *any*thing.

My sister was chasing me and I ran smack into a sharp metal surface and cut my forehead open. I remember standing at the sink in my grandmother's kitchen, while my mother, crying, washed the blood away.

(*Lady Gay*—8.) They had not come to stay. They wanted nothing and could use nothing, being desireless. She sought them later and could not find them.

SHADOWS

Shadows on a dirty street. Bright sun. Children. Sparrows.

Window. Carpet. Window. Carpet. Bed. Window. Carpet. Bed. Sun.

How long to be able to conjure up the image—to raise it, remembered face, in absence? *Memory*, I have opened the book, I have written therein, for the suddenness of a life, or lives, particular, in streets and rooms.

1.

—Of my friendship with Mercury. What do I know of him? In a photograph, he appears from the shadows of a wood, with his arms straight out ahead, his mouth open wide, his long fair hair streaming, and a strange look in his eyes. He seems to have been running straight at the camera. A cloak billows behind him.

We took the train together from London, arriving in Hampshire in the evening. Mercury and I kept repeatedly going down a row of country lanes, and none of them seemed right; or rather, they would seem right at first, but then we still couldn't find the house. It was a winter evening, and very dark, and neither of us had tried to find the place in the night before.

I remember sitting with Flora at the kitchen table in her flat while she showed me various snapshots of her latest holiday, including this strange photograph of a strange man: Mercury.

Flora went through a phase of declaring over and over that poetry was a dead art.—It's finished, she would say, *historically* finished. Mercury and I both being poets, this was provocative. I eventually got fed up and said to Mercury, If she says that poetry is a dead art once more, I'll strangle the bitch.—*You'll* strangle her, he said; like hell: *I'll* strangle her.

A shift from one window to another—there only being two. One, overlooking a small garden at the back of the house; a room in which the bed was a mattress on the floor: I lived there for two years. One evening shortly before this move, I sat with Mercury in the kitchen of the place he was staying in, and talked until it was too late to get a bus home: so I walked back, through the dark streets and across a bridge, and I became strangely joyful. For it was predominantly a sad, a painful time. The other window looks out onto a square of tenements; it also, in projection, looks out onto a river on which a boat glides, through nights of marriage; a gold-reddish light on the waters.

This section is dedicated to Ernst Gombrich.

2.

It was her resemblance to Lucy that first shocked me about a young woman named Chloris. It was not only the physical resemblance (which in fact I probably exaggerated) but also a common interest in that sphere, not of the spirit, but the Will posed as spirit, with attendant esotericism and aristocratic pretensions.

A ring. An edge of light, always moving further down, along the rain-flecked dark shining stones of the alleyway.

O Chloris!—That Zephyr shall never see you again.

In a fine poem called 'The Challenge', John Clarke wrote: "...That Night I/ said If you speak to Her/ She will speak to you because// that was my experience..." This idea, in a different context, also appears in William Godwin's novel *Caleb Williams*. It is dear to me, because it has not been true for me.

On my walks with Mercury and Flora in the country, Flora would rather pedantically point out the plants, trees and flowers and tell us their names. She'd had nothing to do since breaking her leg, so she studied botany and read Russian novels.

Where are the companions, after all? They have gone.

At a reading by a visiting American poet, seeing poets in the audience and knowing them yet not seeing them very often, I was led to reflect on how little I see of *anyone*. One of the poets, Cupid, I don't care to see. He's obsessed with love. He sits and grins at people and doesn't say anything. He's not much of a person, more like half a person, and I shan't say any more about him.

3.

Lucy told me touchingly of how a girl in her dancing class came up to her and silently put her head on Lucy's shoulder.

I came to trust Mercury implicitly. I had got into some bother with Lucy and her husband. I was not in control of my emotions. It was Mercury who unhesitatingly pledged his help, and he was almost the only one.

I had to leave the house I'd lived in for two years. And at first I could find nowhere else to go to. I telephoned Lucy, but she wanted nothing further to do with me and hung up.

Two years previous to this, I'd been staying with a beautiful young woman, tall and slim, with red hair, named Mary, who had also at one time been a dancer. The landlord had complained of my presence in the house, so Mary threw me out.

A more truly sympathetic person was an Italian-Jewish woman named Beatrice, a friend of Mercury's. She would complain that English people were so awkward in their use of their bodies: they had comparatively little feeling for movement and spontaneity. I admit that she never put me up but she did put up a friend of mine.

Lucy, Mary, Beatrice. Strange to think of these three together.

For weeks I've tried to ring my friend Venus, a gentle and lively young woman with a firm belief in hedonism. First she was away for the weekend, then she was on holiday in Amsterdam, and since then she's been out every night for a week.

After having bought a record by Rashied Ali, I went into a shop to get some fish and chips, and the man behind the counter, glancing at the record, asked me if Rashied Ali was an Arab.—No, I said; are you Arabian? Pointing at the man frying the chips, he said, No, but *he* is. This is the only thing in this text which isn't true. It isn't true in the sense that it didn't happen to me. It *did* happen to a friend of mine, however, and I use the incident with his knowledge and permission.

179

4.

If these assemble as in one place and time, it can only throw a light on what is definitely loss; so that these are shadows:

Cupid blinded, to go with the story, poised in the air at the level of the oranges on the trees; whereas I remember him only as seated and smirking moonily. Beneath him, appearing in the centre of the scene, Venus: shyly smiling, her head bowed to the left, and one hand raised in an indeterminate gesture. My memory of her, left wholly to itself, is like two small photographs that alternate rapidly, in one of which the head is, yes, bowed and her smile slight and shy; in the other she has her head lifted and her smile is more forceful. From the right, Flora steps forward boldly, casting flowers onto the ground; her botany studies have affected her in such a way that she communicates her botanical fervour forcefully, physically, to Chloris, who rushes towards her from the far right, as if to melt into her: indeed, leaves appear out of poor Chloris' mouth as she turns her head back to glance at her pursuer, Zephyr. God knows, but perhaps something of Flora's passion for Russian novels has been carried across to Chloris and me as well. As I come swooping down to arrest her flight, looking rather wild and windy, I can distinctly hear Chloris hiss: 'Leave—me—alone!', which causes me to reflect on how much people change their minds about other people.

Next to Venus, on the other side, Lucy, Mary and Beatrice link hands and dance sweetly, gracefully. Mercury, at far left, doesn't come rushing out of the woods with his arms thrust straight out in front of him, hair blowing, mouth open, and cape billowing; instead he looks upward towards a sky hidden by the clustered leaves of the orange trees, and points towards it with his caduceus. If he turns his head full frontal, and speaks now, it is to say three words:

—Continuance; or endurance....

OUT
OF THIS
WORLD

Hurrying across a bridge in the city, with traffic on my right and the river on the left, a woman's face, smiling, detaches from the features surrounding her. Whether memory or trick of memory, I go on, passing her; and yet I have remained, looking.

What separation, then, of heart and body?—Cusanus, who wrote and activated so much for the cause of unity, was given two burials: his heart removed and buried in one place, the rest of his body buried in another.

●

When is it we can die into our true life?

Kneeling on the shining floor, the figure in orange brocade puts one hand to what should be mouth, gap in a white female-mask; small slits for the eyes, and the head bowed for the smooth white surface to touch the hand: a hand too broad, large.

●

Clive had told me about his friend Sandra, who lived near where I did — although, he said, she might in fact have moved since he'd last been in touch with her. One evening Clive turned up on my doorstep with a bottle of brandy and insisted that I help him drink it. He didn't actually *need* any help. In those days at least, Clive seemed to do little else except get drunk, in a circle of despair and bitterness, and intoxication. He asked if I'd like to meet Sandra, warning me, however, that we might find her in bed with someone, as according to Clive she spent much of her time that way.

I had gone to the cinema with Paul and Michael to see a double-bill, the first and best part of which was a Philip Marlowe film. During the interval Sandra, whom I had met for the first time just that morning, came and, oblivious of us, sat down in the row immediately in front. She turned and recognised me, and I introduced her to my companions. She told us she'd seen the coming film five times already. Paul asked her what she liked about it.—I'm very keen on Bertolucci, she said.—Did he have something to do with it? asked Paul.—This is *Last Tango in Paris*?—No, we chorused.—Shit! she said, and ran out of the cinema.

We sat at a street-café opposite the crowded market-place, drinking fruit juice because Sandra couldn't drink alcohol. A writer of our time—a theologian with more understanding of the epoch than a great many of his contemporaries—imaged its possibilities through the medieval festival known as the Feast of Fools, in which social positions were called into question and a joyous anarchy reigned. Yet he saw those possibilities as created by fantasy, rooted in desire; and although this theologian would have wished differently, the desiring ego has in its fundamental constitution the ultimate positing of its own freedom as an absolute, which is to say a pseudo-absolute; in the interests of this absolute freedom or power, all and everything else must be subjected to it. So too Sandra spoke of a Utopian spectacle of profligate desire: how do you tell someone you're not interested in phantasmagoria?—I'm not interested in phantasmagoria. —Fuck *you.*

●

In dream, searching for two girls, their imaged presences breaking in upon temporal absence in the dream; searching in subways, in printed or spoken words, or amongst streets of bright store-fronts at night.

●

Red and pink flowers, in a dense cluster of green above and over earthen-brown pots, are framed by the black space behind and diaphanous grey-white of curtain pulled to the side, making a triangle broken by a double white horizontal (window, raised); colours of the flowers also framed by the white horizontals and verticals, and surrounding white, of frame and wall. Sometimes someone will appear behind the flowers, to tend to them or look—at them or out. Darkness obscures or negates sight of them.

During a famine in a major city, cannibalism appeared on a large scale and the general moral values of the city's culture broke down correspondingly; to see and hear was to doubt the seen and heard for the terror of it: but it was also to hold to a place co-incidentally present, out of this world.

●

Peter challenged my separation of imagination and fantasy, and the low value I put on the latter. He wanted to say that fantasy was of value for the imaging of possibilities it presented; and that the distinction I wished to make between the two was, anyway, rather vague. I said that what I wished to lay stress on was the mode of orientation involved; the participation within that vision of the world which is *sub specie aeternitatis,* which also gave to love and desire their proper orientation.

We had spent some time at Paul's place, talking and drinking together before going to see a film; during that time Clive unexpectedly dropped by to leave some things with Paul. He said hello to both Peter and me, yet it was commonly accepted that Clive and I were definitely not on friendly terms any more, as Clive's incoherent and inarticulate rage at life led him to strike out wherever chance fell, one result of which was a spoof article he wrote attacking me untruthfully as being involved in fascist activities. 1 was not appeased *by* the fact that it was transparently silly. It was an embittered and vicious silliness which could, apart from a certain type of cowardice, have led him just as easily to physically attack someone or act in any other destructive way. He also tried to posit a comic radicalism for what he was doing in such an article, which *was* comic in as much as Clive had no commitment to anything and was quite apolitical, so that any so-called radicalism he might pretend to by play-acting the *enfant terrible* was grounded only in despair of commitment, muddle-mindedness, and a concomitant perverseness.

The following afternoon Peter and I took a walk in a park, followed by lunch at a neighbourhood café; then we went to the train-station where he was to catch a train back home. Coming away, I thought of what I had told Sandra, that strange to say never in my life had I bought flowers for anyone.

•

Eyes fixed in intensity. Cheeks drawn in, the eyes narrowed, he kneels to the shining floor. Or standing straight, one knee raised, fist clenching a fan held straight out in front. Who wrote: "It's not flashy, almost nothing on the surface; it's *inside* or not at all..."

The figure kneels, one hand holding a fan which almost touches the shining floor; the other is raised to cover the mouth of a smooth white mask, and the hand poised against this white surface shows itself as large, broad.

Wooden sandals, such as Buddhist nuns wear, and in the background a fire.

Amongst the various images presented on a television screen, *one* image detaching itself, perception unwilling, that this *is* a man, a monk sitting quite still in the flames; then as the painful recognition settles, he falls sideways to the ground. "And then", someone wrote, "people who deal in destruction as art, will try to claim a death such as this on behalf of their own 'radicalism', and write about it in their art journals: crows feeding on the brave dead; shallow, stupid, and frivolous to the last."

•

First Gary went home, and then his friend Lionel stopped seeing me.

Noel arrived; we'd not seen each other for six years; I was as shocked by the changes in him, as I was glad to have his company again.

I gave Noel the name *Orestes,* because like that Greek hero he suffered into truth. But equally, just as Ruskin had, however pretentiously, called Dante Gabriel Rossetti a great Italian lost in the Inferno of London, I could characterise Noel as a noble Australian lost—hopelessly lost—in that same Inferno.

One day Noel went back home also. The same old story.

•

Paul and I were sitting in his tiny room—there was scarcely room enough for us, the bed, chair, miniature television, record-player, books and records—when there were loud noises from the bathroom next door. Paul went to investigate, and found Noel, who lived in a room one flight down, with a metal shower-rail in his hand and an appreciable hole in the plaster wall.— Noel, what's wrong? he asked. Noel, one of the gentlest of people, looked over his shoulder at Paul and said simply, Nothing.

When I was in my late teens, living in Melbourne, Noel was, as a slightly older man possessing creative talent, someone I looked up to. At that time he was studying art at a technical college, first part- and later full- time. I would go to his house to look at his paintings and drawings. There were a few drawings, but very few paintings; and none of them were ever "finished" in a conventional sense; Noel would bring them to a certain point, and then leave them. His painting-teachers were apparently bemused and not particularly pleased by this habit—for I think it was a habit or a character-trait to which any deliberate artistic intention was subsidiary. I felt a good deal of enthusiasm for Noel's work.

When Noel left London, he gave me a drawing in pen and wash of three bottles. It was one of the few successful drawings—and he had done very few drawings at all, successful or not, and only one abortive painting—of this eighteen-month-stay. Different views of the bottles were superimposed but also condensed so that each bottle was *one* yet *more than* one. Like those paintings of Noel's I had known years before, there was a faithfulness to familiar things and at the same time a piercing of that familiarity: a penetration, I felt, to a more fundamental view which brought the familiar into question. For this reason, the drawing was reminiscent of Giacometti's paintings and, equally, of Giorgio Morandi.

•

Sandra had told me of a writers' group which met once a week in a house very near where we both lived. To be sociable I said I'd go there with her; even though I've come by experience to distrust such groups. Standing on the steps of this house, 1 asked Sandra if she knew of an Irish-Canadian writer of poetic prose, someone I'd never discussed with anyone before, and surprisingly she did. His work was typical of a mode of writing in Britain which developed in the 40s, and which was centred upon subjectivity, and predominantly upon desire and private pain, and upon hyperbolic simile. However, unlike a couple of much better known writers of this mode, whose work was essentially characterised by selfishness, desire and pain in this man's work were caught up in a movement of generosity, of universal sympathy.

I had once, several years before, found my way to the house where this writer lived, in a London slum, but had been told by his landlady that he was away in Ireland.

Sandra rang the doorbell of this other house, and we were let in, but as we climbed the stairs I changed my mind about wanting to go in, and took my leave of her.

●

Two little girls: one of them, clinging to a pole near a garden wall, smiles and waves at me as I walk past on the opposite side of the road.

Red flowers, crowned by a small number of white, and surrounded by large green leaves below, are framed by the white verticals and horizontals of the window and surrounding white of the wall; behind them, a green drape hanging at one side breaks the prevailing darkness.

Gary had come over to England on a writing-grant, and being the friend of a friend, he dropped by my place and introduced himself. Shortly afterwards, he came around with a friend named Lionel, who was working as an actor in a children's theatre group at the time but clearly had better things in mind for himself as far as the acting profession was concerned. Lionel had previously been a teacher, and had become an advocate of A.S. Neill's ideas about education and, through Neill, Reich's notions about sexuality and society. He clearly saw himself as a revolutionary of sorts. Gary and Lionel were to go to a party in the evening, and they invited me to join them. Dick, a friend of Noel's who was staying with me, came along with us. Dick was to establish himself as an unlovely person, telling malicious gossip to mutual friends back in Melbourne amongst other things. But at the time, he seemed to us a nice enough, if unintelligent, sort of person. (Noel must have had the same idea.) The party was a listless affair. Dick went outside to "look at the stars", and a little later Lionel went out to help him look at them. Gary commented that he thought it a rather romantic situation. The insinuation was clear, (and later other people made similar comments), but for a person like Lionel whose profession of heterosexuality was reinforced by his advocacy of Reichian bias, it was a good bit strange. Combined with middle-class dress and manners, his "revolutionary" attitudes similarly seemed ironic, as did his idealistic fervour for such a predominantly reactionary sphere of existence as the British theatre-world.

Lionel and I were for many months on the best of terms; we saw each other often, and at one time considered sharing a flat together. Then, following an argument with a girl-friend which Lionel witnessed, he sent me a short note saying he'd never considered that we had anything in common, and that he wanted nothing further to do with me.

●

I had written a short book on a novelist who had slowly destroyed himself with alcohol; I had said as little as possible about the alcoholism, preferring to concentrate on his actual work as a writer. Clive reviewed my book entirely in terms of that man's self-destruction, and said nothing about his texts, nor mine. When Clive showed me the review, I asked him not to publish it. Later, sitting in a café, he said to me, smiling, You *were* interested in him because he was self-destructive, weren't you? And isn't it because *you're* like that, too!

A postcard from Clive, again pretending a link on my part with fascism, and signed, "Love, Bugs Bunny".

●

When Noel first arrived, he was considerably shaken by events that had recently taken place in Melbourne. Dick had gone off with the woman Noel was in love with, and from what Noel claimed, Dick, the woman, and two brothers who knew Dick and Noel, deliberately tried to cause Noel as much unhappiness as possible. I think he had probably been in a rather unstable way before that happened. But he had been pushed to the verge of an emotional collapse. I shan't even try to guess all that was wrong, although I tried to find out what I could in order to help him as much as possible. "The real reasons that make or break a man are too absurd or too obscene to be reached from outside."

•

Red and pink flowers, in a dense cluster of green, above and over earthen-brown pot, are framed by the black space behind and diaphanous grey-white of curtain pulled to the side, making a triangle broken by a double white horizontal (window, raised); colours of the flowers also framed by the white horizontals and verticals, and surrounding white, of frame and wall. Sometimes someone will appear behind the flowers, to tend to them or look—at them or out. Darkness obscures or negates sight of them.

Wooden sandals, such as Buddhist nuns wear, and in the background, a fire.

SCRAPS

She said, You probably won't believe this, but I really liked you very much; immediately leaving the table and going out the door. I sat there feeling a little dazed by the suddenness of this appeal to friendship; should I have gone after her and said something?

•

My sister and I were amongst several children invited by the older girls who lived in the house opposite ours to come by for a puppet show one afternoon. I think I was more impressed by coming inside this otherwise unavailable domain itself than by the shadow-world created by the girls' puppetry; those girls would not ordinarily have spoken to us at all: and this was thorough-going: we were invited, at the end of the little show, to come for another performance if and when we could bring entrance-money. We never saw that interior again.

Twenty-one years of age, walking by water's side; river flowing, dirty, past industrial slums, grimy walls of factories; debris and mud everywhere. I had just been to an interview for a job I didn't want, and despite all my attempts at not getting accepted, it looked like

I had been anyway: *what* a disappointment. Actually, I wasn't just disappointed, I felt sick. Some gulls flew over; and I thought of the young woman at the labour exchange who had sent me to the interview. Her face came into focus: an attractive woman; stylish; probably a nice person. Maybe she'd go far in her job. I was going to leave the country.

•

I hadn't heard from my friend Paul for some time, so I phoned him up: How have you been? I asked. He said he'd been in bed the last few days.—Why, I asked, what was wrong with you?—I was in a speechless rage, he said.

•

White semi-circle with a blurred outline of yellow/ cut across by blood-red clouds: ensign, insignia? A sign, certainly.

—I am proud, the old man said; I am proud of the beautiful decorations in my offices; I have been given an award because of the beauty of these decorations. Working in such surroundings, my employees are happier, more docile. Not only do the surroundings contribute to this. Every month we have a ceremony. We pray to our ancestors and to the divine spirit.

•

I'd taken a job as an attendant at an administrative centre belonging to a Protestant organization, The Society of Friends. I was supposed to interrogate everyone who came into the building to make sure they were not a potential thief; presumably the Friends had a good deal of trouble with thieves. I didn't do my job. I found a piano in the recesses of the building, and spent as much time as possible trying out figures on it. I was also supposed to keep tramps out. There were many tramps in the neighbourhood. This was especially a problem in the evenings: apparently, they could be discovered lying around in out-of-the-way places, and you were supposed to go looking with a flash-light, routing them from the building. This sounded like an undesirable sort of operation to me. So I asked an acquaintance to help me with the night-duty, paying him a cut of my meagre salary for his help. He was a young man, in his early twenties, who wore a Native American head-band. 1 suspected him of being quietly psychotic. He would search around while I sat and hammered at the keyboard. If he ever succeeded in finding any bodies, he had the good sense not to tell me about it.

After I'd come back from a holiday in Greece, I was given a new position at the Society: I was henceforth a janitor in the toilets. This new position also involved sorting through all the trash collected from the offices, by hand, and separating the paper from everything else—used tea-bags, cigarette-butts, dirty Kleenex, and so forth. The paper then had to be made up into bales bound with iron wire. This was all done in a tiny room in the basement, behind the boiler-room. There was a fragment of rope hanging from a metal ceiling-beam; the man who had been my predecessor had hung himself in the room.

This demotion effected a display of snobbery from most of the administrative staff, who formerly would at least have said hello. I got used to eating by myself in the staff canteen. That is, until a young Scottish woman with a very lively and friendly way started to make it a habit of sitting with me at lunch. She talked and talked—unfortunately because of her accent I could sometimes only barely get the gist of her conversation; it seemed to be mainly to do with drinking, boyfriends, and domestic chaos. I advised her in my best avuncular manner to go easy on the booze and boys. One day I told her that I'd given notice. I was surprised to see how she was saddened by this news.

Walking into the outer courtyard of the building, I looked across into the distance of figures and buildings and traffic.

•

Paul had been working in the cosmetics and toiletry section of a large department-store; he was fired for putting a bar of their soap in his coat-pocket. When he lost the job, somehow it seemed as if the bottom fell out of his life. He found himself unable to tell his parents he was no longer working there; and he conceived the idea that he had become unemployable. At about the same rime he struck up a romance with a young woman who worked in a pizza restaurant. It was a sort of minimalist romance; Paul told me they weren't spoiling things by holding hands or anything like that. Then he had to leave the room he'd been living in because the landlord put up the rent. Finally his waitress friend disappeared from her job and he never saw her again.

There was a huge window on the top floor, and you could see the river and a part of the city across the river. At sunset the red sun was shattered on the waters, a sustained crash of percussion. I distributed mail in this building several times a day, and took mail from the offices over to another building belonging to the same firm. It wasn't much of a job, and I was made to appreciate the insignificance of my position: both my immediate superiors and the other workers ignored me as much as possible. No, jumping *out* the window would have been going *too* far. But each day I kept thinking that if I could fake a collapse, and be found spread-eagled on the shining linoleum outside the metal-doors of the elevators on that top floor, where the huge window overlooked the river, 1 could be taken off sick for the day. Could I have done it convincingly enough? No; *they'd* have smelled me out.

She said, You probably won't believe this, but I really liked you very much; immediately leaving the table and going out the door. I sat there feeling a little dazed by the suddenness of this appeal to friendship; should I have gone after her and said something? It was already too late. I left the job that same afternoon—well before I'd been due to. Walking into the outer courtyard of the building, I looked across into the distance of figures and buildings and traffic. Some birds flew overhead. Images formed and re-formed like *an archaeology of cinema*: sadness, fragmented nobility. Colours of cars going by, dresses of women walking past, silver glints of light from the windows of the buildings. Scraps.

...going on the floor, but then dialing a little more to
the audience... of this speed to transition... should I've
also gone that he's in and and sunshine? It was already
to a corner. I think job can stop the ground as with slow
to one side in Walking into the other. outward little
building. I didn't agree, onto the elements of figure
and buildings and the time... some back new overhead in
things... I met and returned this... on to Twelve of...
in the distance. Fragmented mobility the one of bars
sitting by another and wonderwork little part also right
on right from the windows of the building. Source

BLUES

There was a crashing sound, and I ran up the stairs and turned the red handle of the door; entering the room, I saw that the windowpane had been smashed. Directly below the window was a new painting, which I'd left on the floor to dry.

—What about Annabel, I had asked my mother a week before; do you still see her?—Oh, she's dead, my mother said.—But how? How did she die?—I don't know, she said.

•

Two figures run through a park at night, around a fountain and amongst the trees: hide-and-seek; hallucinatory running-speeds—and moments of stillness (they stop; laughing at each other). This could be a dream, but it is not. These figures course death in flash after flash.

•

Annabel wrote me a letter, which I could hardly understand at all; and of which I remember almost nothing: I wish I had it with me now. She had become very religious at that time and had written to remind me of my own "most real nature"; that much I can remember. I can also remember a distressing incident she recounted in the letter. One night she was awoken by, she said, God's voice speaking to her. She thought she was being called to go out into the streets in search of her God, in the flesh; but when she did so, she was set upon by a couple of drunks, who tried to rape her. I can't remember any more of what the letter said.

•

As we walked down the stone steps, John told me how he had found there, once, the contents of a woman's handbag, scattered as if in a struggle. He'd discovered, amongst the rest, a letter with the address of a job, but when he enquired at that place they had not known of the woman.

In the car, the woman lay unmoving in the man's arms. A cop stood at the open window.

The sea was calm; we leaned against the iron-mesh of the barrier, and looked across the body of water to the lights on the opposite shore.

•

I had to spend the day at college carrying a travelling-case from room to room; I'd been unable to take it home before going in that morning. A fellow student, when I happened to phone him the following day, said that when I'd been observed with the case, it'd been assumed I was going away. Then I found myself attempting to speak to him about her, the woman Elspeth, and to no avail.

•

The evening before I was to leave for Australia, Elspeth telephoned me.

I remembered another time: leaning in a doorway, waiting until she had come up to where I stood. We talked there for a short time; she broke off the conversation by saying that her children would be standing in the cold at the bus-shelter where she collected them, and that if she were late they'd tell me she was a "bad mother".

When I confessed to fears about the trip to Australia, she said that was only natural: you had to expect that

213

by the time of entering the plane everything would blur and start swimming.

•

From the prevailing darkness, a silver-green edge— of a metal tray, set on the table—shines from the doorway. I was worried about the amount of blood I was passing with my urine; if it kept up, I'd have to go back to the hospital.

•

Driving over the bridge, I looked out the window to see a flock of gulls wheeling across the sky, the darkness riding them.

On one occasion, John had caught the last ferry for the evening and found himself the only passenger aboard. He described the event as something strangely joyous, but there came to my mind Melville's dream of Edgar Poe, as a lone man standing on the deck of a half-wrecked boat at sea. A short distance from our station at the waters, there was a small stone fountain, broken and hence disused, in a lonely pond.—There's a clock

without hands, not far, he said; it's disturbing.—I feel
that here, I said. So we walked away.

●

I was left alone in my friend's studio, with the
heavy slabs of coloured glass standing against the
walls, the sketches pinned up, and paintings stacked
one against another.

Dreams moving over an ocean's plenitude. Extremity,
in which one waits, attendant upon what is unknown.
But this is desire and love. I, hopelessly, am waiting.

●

I was probably fourteen, so she would have been
about thirty-nine. She had stayed at our house
overnight; much to the reluctance of my mother, who
warned me not to use a particular towel, as Annabel
had used it, and she was "dirty". After Annabel had
left, I went upstairs by myself; standing in the empty
bathroom with her image in my mind, I said: I love you.

It was a half an hour too early when I arrived at the station, so instead of catching a bus the rest of the distance, I decided to walk. At half-seven it was already dark, and the air was cold.

Once, I had stepped into a train-carriage, on the way to a film-show, and had found Elspeth standing there. The film included footage of ceremonial dancing by some African tribesmen, dressed in costumes made of feathers. The audience laughed at these images; their laughter annoyed me. I was reminded, strangely, of the mating-ritual of a certain water bird, which performs complex, ballet-like actions across the surface of the water, with rapid linear movements and sudden turns.

I came to the door and rang the bell; Elspeth's oldest child, a girl of thirteen, opened the door to me.

•

She was probably the gentlest person I have ever known. (Thinking of her now, late at night, in the rain, as I wait for a taxi—remembering how she wouldn't take a black-painted taxi home from my parents', because to her black signified death.)

•

When I saw John again, at a bookshop where we had arranged by phone to meet, it was eight years since we had last seen each other. (I cannot even remember the circumstances of that last meeting. In the intervening years we had kept in touch, if intermittently, by letter.) We later went back to John's home, and it being evening by then, he went into his children's bedroom to say goodnight to them.—Daddy, said one of them, what are you doing here?—I *live* here, he said, laughing. Sitting in the living-room, drinking coffee, I noticed a large painting on the wall, which reminded me of the work of an English Pop artist, Richard Hamilton.—Who's the painter? I asked.—Oh, he's not really a painter, John said in his quiet, measured voice; he's a framer. He does some collage and some "fool-the-eye" effects, that sort of thing…. He shrugged.—People liked the first one he did, so he continued doing them, and even gets commissions now. After a pause, he added: He's a good frame-maker, though.

·

John sent me an essay by the Anglo-Sri Lankan writer Ananda Coomaraswamy; in which I found the following quotation: "When my heart beheld Love's sea, of a sudden it left me and leapt in."

·

She told me of her experience, as a child, of the darkness, the terror of dark spaces, of how it had stayed with her, and had come into the light of the present as something that she must recognise and deal with.

I had seen her many times, noticed her in the refectory at lunch (sometimes with her children), passed her in corridors and in the college library; and this for a long time.

I was sitting in a new class, when she came in, late after taking her children to school, and sat down, beside me.

DREAM
IMAGES
OF LIFE

The samurai Jirō Naozane, because of dissatisfaction with his relations with the Shōgun, became a priest under the name Rensei and before long a disciple of Hōnen. Hōnen on their first meeting told Rensei that to attain salvation all he need do was to recite the *Nembutsu*, or sacred invocation (*Namu Amida Butsu*). Amida Buddha's Vow, he said, was to save all those who earnestly called upon his name. At this Rensei burst into uncontrollable tears. When Hōnen at length asked him why he wept so, he answered: I supposed you would tell me I should have to cut off my hands and feet and give up my life if I would be saved.... *Simplicity*: what was it? What did it mean? The two men walked down to the Harbour and stood looking out over the dark calm water while one told the other of an evening when he had caught the last ferry, alone. They walked back by way of a small park where there was a broken fountain, the water still and stagnant. *Nembutsu*-followers were said to be reborn, after their death, on a lotus in a Pure Land in the West; Rensei made a vow that he wouldn't accept rebirth in the Pure Land unless it was in the highest rank of the highest class of that land. He had a dream which reassured him about this attainment:

he was standing with ten others around a golden lotus flower, and he said to them: No one but myself can get up on that flower; at which he found himself sitting on top of it. Rensei was the headman of his district and if he thought any man guilty of bad conduct, he would make him carry a heavy horsetrough on his back or fetter him hand and foot.

•

Once when Hōnen went to visit the Regent Kanezane—a devout follower of whom Hōnen was to say, We have had an affinity for each other from a former life—Rensei insisted on going along. While Hōnen spoke to the Regent, Rensei waited outside. Not being able to hear the sermon that was being delivered, Rensei exclaimed loudly: What a hatefully vile world is this anyway. Surely Paradise must be vastly different from this. Hearing his words, Kanezane had him invited inside. First one room, then another, window, window, light on a glass bowl of flowers, light on a glass bowl of fruit. Traffic outside; pavement, trees. He pared down to the core. Cool fire of light off burnished steel: the inner body was as if a minimalist sculpture, a streamlined bird of aspiration. Rensei said, Birth into the Land of Bliss is a reward which belongs to the future, and is still far distant. And yet here I am thus quickly entering upon the enjoyment of it here and now in the present, when I am allowed to come right inside such a palace as this. Surely no one could attain the like except by the practice of the *Nembutsu*, as the Original Vow prescribed.

●

Rensei wrote of a strange dream: "...I saw a slender golden lotus with an elongated stem without any branches on it, growing out of the ground. Around it stood some ten persons, to whom I addressed the following words—'No one but myself can get up on that flower.' No sooner had I said this than, without knowing how I did it, I found myself sitting on it, and with that I awoke." She sat back in the chair, in the centre of the room, and lit a cigarette. Light on the right side of her face. Dark, soft hair. Rensei said, I have had dreams over and over again of being born into the highest rank of the highest class. Regent Kanezane wrote to Hōnen about the reputation Rensei was gaining because of the wonderful omens he received in his dreams: "...

everything connected with this man is passing strange. I can hardly keep the tears back at the very thought of him."

●

The samurai Jirō Naozane had distinguished himself in battle as a warrior; but due to poor relations with the Shōgun, Naozane became a priest under the name of Rensei. He was advised to call on Hōnen to ask his advice on some questions relating to the afterlife. She told him of how on a weekend in the country with some others, she'd had a fit of crying and been comforted by another young woman. She'd been subject to such outbursts for about ten years, that is, since her midteens, as if they compensated for or expressed some emotional frustration. Or rather she said, to do with love. More and more he wandered streets to hold nothing; eyeing women passing by or sitting in restaurants, shops, offices. Hōnen wrote to Rensei: "It is a terrible fact that devils always get in the way of those who are striving for Buddhahood, and so you want to be on your guard. This is why I call your attention to this fact, for auspicious as these wonderful omens must be, it is possible that evil spirits will try to take advantage

of them to lead you astray, and so you will do well to
be very circumspect, and be much in prayer to Amida."

•

Once when Hōnen went to visit the Regent
Kanezane, Rensei insisted on accompanying him.
While Hōnen spoke to the Regent, Rensei waited
outside. Not being able to hear the words of Hōnen's
sermon, Rensei exclaimed loudly, What a hatefully vile
world is this anyway. Surely Paradise must be vastly
different than this. He stood at the top of the stairs. At
the bottom was the kitchen, in the kitchen there would
be a knife. He would take the knife into the bathroom
and lock the door. He felt bad about doing it in her flat,
but then everything felt bad. He thought of an incident
some years previous, when he'd been surprised with a
knife at his wrist in the kitchen of a house he shared
with several other people. He heard the door open and
close again. He was still standing at the top of the stairs.
Light on the right side of her face. Kanezane had Rensei
brought in. Rensei said, Birth into the Land of Bliss is
a reward which belongs to the future, and is still far
distant. And yet here I am thus quickly entering upon
the enjoyment of it here and now in the present, when

I am allowed to come right inside such a palace as this. Surely no one could attain the like except by the practice of the *Nembutsu,* as the Original Vow prescribed.

•

Details of the life were pared away to construct the essential: "Not this", "Not that." Worried about his state of mind, she made up a bed for herself on the living-room floor and gave him her own bed. When he went into the bedroom he found he couldn't stay—there were photographs of other men, and letters he jealously examined, as well as posters which he couldn't help finding vulgar. He opened the door to the living-room and said her name... and said that he had to leave. So she told him to turn the light on; and he let himself out. Once in the street, he equally couldn't face walking all the way home in the cold night. The samurai Saburō Tanemori came into contact with Hōnen when he was thirty-three and immediately became a disciple. After Hōnen died, Tanemori grew more and more sick of the world and wished to join Hōnen in Paradise. One night he slashed open his stomach and took out his entrails, wrapping them in a pair of silk trousers to be thrown into the river. She sat back in the chair, legs crossed, hands around her knee. Light on the right side of her face.—I shall never see you again, and you'll never know, nor will I.... They sat in silence for a time. Then she said: Will you take care of yourself? He looked away, at the white wall. After a while he said: You've had nothing to offer. Nothing except sentimental sympathy.... At the door there was nothing to say. In the subway he walked round and round, completely lost, unable to get a grip on himself. As he walked past the stream of people hurrying towards home from their jobs, he felt sick with remorse; as if the present state of his life were final.

THERE AND HERE:
A meditation
on
Gérard de Nerval

It's said that Gérard was still breathing when first come upon, but nobody wanted to interfere and cut him down; by the time the police arrived he was quite dead. A friend, describing his death, wrote of "that abominable street, the witness of a lonely agony". And he continues: "At the back of the narrow fissure, a pale ray caught the golden figure of Renown on the fountain in the Place du Châtelet and made it gleam like some vague symbol of glory...."

*

For Gérard, remembrance was pictured by the myosotis or forget-me-not; it was (and is) constancy, and he saw the star of love, healer of souls, dwelling upon it as an insistence or endurance, an enduring light. It grew where there is ascent. The pearl, too, which some traditions have imaged as a cure for insanity and melancholia: this was remembrance's figure. Like the alchemists' elixir, the pearl was associated with the moon, and has been used in the symbolism both of Saviourhood and of the Immaculate Conception. Combined with the Rose, symbolic of the

Virgin, of beauty, and of the femininity-ideal: the Rose Pearl; which resides at the centre of "the holy table, made of the seven most precious metals"; the metals of the alchemist, gold, silver, copper, tin, iron, lead, and quicksilver. And here in the soul, the Alchemical Work takes place: the first two stages are designated by black and white: darkness or descent, and purification or ascent—"By means of putrefaction, fermentation, and trituration—all of which take place in darkness— the *materia* is divested of its initial form. By means of bleaching to a silvery white it is purified."

It is the Rose Pearl, Gerard said, which resisted the hammer-blow of pride, *hubris* of fire and forge— the hammer-blow which broke the holy table, and attempted to break the world. But Gérard was under the protection of Apollo, god of poetry and of medicine; and like Adonis he was beloved of Aphrodite.

*

Aurélia had been "sleeping in some palace", some other existence, where Gérard, here, could not reach her.

When questioned about his love for Aurélia, Gérard replied that he only pursued an *image* (or *likeness*). "Seen at close quarters, the real woman revolted our ingenuous souls. She had to be queen or goddess; above all, she had to be unapproachable." (In the notes made during his journey to the Middle East, he mentions searching for the features of one woman in those of others.) Gérard saw in Aurélia a trans-psychosis—the carrying-over of the soul's attributes from one person to another—of the already idealised figure from childhood, Adrienne. Gérard significantly invoked Dante in his beautiful description of the encounter with Adrienne:

I was the only boy in the round, and I had brought with me my young companion, Sylvie... I loved her alone, she was the only one I had eyes for—until then! In the round we were dancing I had barely noticed a tall, lovely, fair-haired girl they called Adrienne. All at once, in accordance with the rules of the dance, Adrienne and I found ourselves alone in the centre of the circle. We were of the same height. We were told to kiss and the dancing and the chorus whirled around us more quickly than ever. As I gave her this kiss I could not resist pressing her hand. The long tight curls of her golden hair brushed my cheeks and from that moment on an inexplicable confusion took hold of me.

....

As Adrienne sang, the shadows came down from the great trees, and the first moonlight fell on her as she stood alone in our attentive circle. She stopped, and no one dared to break the silence. The lawn was covered with thin veils of vapour which trailed white tufts on the tips of the grasses. We imagined we were in paradise. Finally I got up and ran to the gardens of the chateau, where some laurels grew, planted in large faïence vases with monochrome bas-reliefs. I brought back two branches which were then woven into a crown and tied with a ribbon. This I put on Adrienne's head and glistening leaves shone on her fair hair in the pale moonlight. She was like Dante's Beatrice, smiling on the poet as he strayed on the verge of the blessed abode.

The woman-as-Ideal can only be approached where the self becomes as nothing so that the other becomes all; but this is an implied criticism, in that there can be no proper balance. Certainly neither are presented in terms of human beings in an equal relationship. Aurélia could only be Gérard's in death. He could only be with her in the dream, in madness, and in death.

'Do you remember death continually?'

'Yes', said Gérard.

'The thirteenth?'

'Yes', said Gérard.

'The boat anchored outside?'

'Yes', said Gérard.

'Who shall untie these knots of the heart?'

'You dance for me alone', said Gérard; 'kiss-me-in-the-ring: head inclined, with one hand holding up—a veil.'

*

In Novalis' unfinished novel *The Disciples at Saïs,* there is a passage in which the dream took over his life, preceded by an expectation of death. An other life. And yet how? It concerns a sorrowful and incompetent young disciple of the Master who one day goes out and, returning late, brings joyfully an oddly-shaped stone, which the Master then places amongst a pattern of stones which intersects with the images of our sensible, that is, waking life. Gérard: "Our dreams are a second life": compare Norman Malcolm's *Dreaming,* where he asserts that to say in a dream we had such-and-such an experience or did this thing or that, is by definition to say that we didn't have the experience or do the thing in question. Rather the dream is a set of images or apparitions amongst a pattern of stones that has already been formed, "just at the point where many lines converged. Never shall I forget that moment. It was as though we had transitorily caught into our souls a clear vision of this wondrous world." Novalis sums up the matter in a simple phrase: "(awareness) of the interrelation of all things, of conjunctions, of coincidence."

Arthur Symons strikes this same note when he remarks of Gérard's writings that they "uncovered the hidden links of divergent things". Constantly death is associated with the Dream ("The first moments of sleep are an image of death") and that strange existence in which the Dream took over his life, preceded by an expectation of death: ("...I began searching the sky for a star I thought I knew as having some influence on my fate. When I had found it I went on walking, following the streets from which it was visible, walking, as it were, towards my destiny, anxious to see the star up to the moment when death would strike me down.")

*

'To the East', said Gérard when asked, just prior to the first attack of madness, where he was going. He told a companion who had appropriately taken "on the aspect of an Apostle": '(I don't) belong to your Heaven. Those in that star are waiting for me. They went before the revelation you have announced to me. Let me go to them, for the one I love belongs to them, and it is there we are to meet again'. In certain Middle Eastern beliefs, as well as in native paganism and occultism, Gérard found the ideas which could better act as a framework to support his Ideal projection of the desires which haunted him. Explicitly opposed to Christianity. In the sonnet 'Artemis' he wrote: "White roses, fall! you offend our gods, / Fall, white phantoms, from your burning heaven: / –The saint of the pit is stronger in my eyes!" When this opposition later changes to an acceptance, it is syncretic and heterodox. With the assistance of the fellow-sufferer he has befriended, Saturninus (this name given by Gérard is the name of a Gnostic teacher of the first century AD), Gérard is able to ride with Aurélia and Christ beyond death, through the *pearly* gates of the New Jerusalem. "It was then", he writes, "that I came down among men to give them the glad tidings", having seen "heaven open in all its glory" and having "read the word *forgiveness* written in Christ's blood." The Corybants can emerge from the secrecy of Gérard's heart into the openness of Christ's love; the world-serpent itself "is slackening its coils", under the influence of the alchemical sulphur and sun, which is to say, the Spirit.

*

At the end of the book bearing her name, Aurélia is the *similitude* and *instrument* of Grace; she is also Isis, speaking in terms reminiscent of the vision in *The Golden Ass;* and she is Gérard's love, Jenny Colon, in as far as Jenny is *contained* in the figure of Aurelia.

How to heal the disparity between the piteous self-abasement in the love-letters to Jenny Colon, wherein it would not be hard to detect emotional masochism, and the presentation of the central figure in *Aurélia?* And yet, the self-abasement is *equal* in these cases, whatever the difference in level....

*

Arrested for his eccentric behaviour (chiefly, undressing in the street), Gérard, lying on a camp-bed, experienced a strange self-bifurcation, projection, so that he became aware of his Double (Doppelgänger —literally "double-walker") in the room. Then he remembered the German tradition that speaks of the Doppelgänger as a sign of one's own imminent death. He thought he saw two friends come for him but take the Double in his stead, and he cried out to them, to no avail; in the morning these very friends did come, but denied having been there during the night.

It was only a few days after this that Gérard had to be taken to an asylum; it was in various mental institutions, at various times, that the dreams that form the bulk of *Aurélia* came.

Though he later learnt of Aurélia's death, which makes it seem that the death that had been adumbrated had really been hers, and not his own, Gérard in entering this "second world" underwent a type of death.

*

Gérard's care for 'Saturninus', a young man in the asylum, catatonic, neither eating nor drinking, served to heal his separation from human life; it broke him from "the monotonous circle of (his) own sensations or moral sufferings". (Gérard's relation to Saturninus reminds me of Bill Plantagenet's concern for the boy and the old man in the asylum in Malcolm Lowry's *purgatorio*-sketch, *Lunar Caustic*. 'It also seems strange to me,' says Plantagenet, 'that I should have to come all the way from England to a madhouse (in America) to find two people I really care about.') Saturninus, in the last page of the book, tells Gérard that he (Saturninus) is already deceased and buried, and undergoing expiation in Purgatory. Gérard comments: "Such are the odd ideas that come with that sort of sickness; I recognised that I myself had not been far from just such a strange belief. (...) I compare this series of trials I went through to that ordeal which, for the ancients, represented the idea of a descent into hell."

Early in his career Gérard had come under the influence of the German Romantic writer and composer E T A Hoffmann, whose eccentric tales dwell on supernatural, occult, and often macabre happenings; importantly, in the light of Gérard's later obsessions, Hoffmann wrote on the Doppelgänger theme. S A Rhodes tells us in his biography of Gérard that the young poet wrote a story, under Hoffmann's influence, on the subject of soul-exchange: a student's soul is exchanged with that of an evil friend, but eventually saved; and that he translated Hoffmann's *Die Serapionsbrüder,* in which there occurs an extra-mundane intervention by Saint-Rosalie to save the heroine Aurélia, who is later murdered out of jealousy by the hero's evil twin brother; Aurélia, dying, charges the story's hero to repentance. In this we have in embryonic form some of the themes encountered in *Aurélia.*

*

The deepening late blue of sky appearing in the window-frame; blue juxtaposed with the green of curtains; blue, for nothing in glory, undiminished by the dirty surface of glass. Walking in Amsterdam—a sign reading 'AURORA' stopped me. I remembered what I had not remembered for years: the name I had given to the heroine of an early prose text, taken from the title of Boehme's *Aurora* just as Gérard had taken the name Aurélia from a story by Hoffmann.

*

In my own early prose texts I worked, out of Nerval and Lowry, with coincidence of events ("the linking-up of things") as the subject-matter, and with juxtapositions, interrelational linking or cutting, as "method". At the same time as this (1971 to 1972) I worked on a long essay on Nerval's work, especially on the images in *Aurélia*; and on a shorter essay on Lowry, which I revised for publication after coming to London in 1972.

In terms of working operations, I tended towards a direct handling of material, cutting up my texts and taping them back together in different combinations. With the Nerval essay, I depended upon chance findings in books I would take almost at random within a limited area of selection, from the shelves of the library at Melbourne University.

*

Without any warning, G— came and sat at our table in the Café Au Montmartre in Tottenham Court Road. My friend asked her about her dervish dancing lessons: Do you really whirl about? She said, No; she hadn't got that far yet. My friend and I moved on to the subject of coincidence—marvellous happening—in writing, as subject and as method. I talked about my apprenticeship as a writer, in Malcolm Lowry and Gérard de Nerval. Breton's *Nadja* and the *I Ching* came into the conversation too; though I have never really concerned myself with either, to be honest (which I wasn't). We had put the woman into a distance, which was a fake distance (I knew exactly where she was). "And through the glass window shines the sun": 6.15 of a winter evening, London, 30/10/75.

*

We were in a Greek restaurant in Notting Hill, and she was questioning me about the origins of my depression. What could I have said? That I grew up in a place that would make anyone aware of other possibilities depressed. Or that I grew up in a family whose members had almost no friends, in a household situated over a small brass-foundry that was operated solely by my father. Within that family I became conditioned to a brooding loneliness which I have never broken out of. Should I mention my early reading, the fact that I was immediately drawn to Nerval and Hölderlin, poets of loss and madness, whose visions helped to consolidate my own approach to a horizon, and the nature of that horizon? I am already sick of this particular story. I will only mention, for what it's worth, that I ended up telling my friend that I wouldn't be seeing her again. A terrible argument followed. And that leads to another story again.

*

"I have tried very hard", she wrote, "to understand and to destroy the barriers I have, naturally, against you (not because you are you but because you are another human being), but I can't do it, because I know you have so many weapons with which to wound me (and you do not use them sparingly). Only a fool or a total idealist throws himself into battle with no armour and no weapons and he probably gets destroyed."

The image. Upside-down, you're laughing; the

motion of the swing's caught. The image caught:
irresistibly; laughter in a face, an image catching me
transversely; the motion of the swing caught, forwards,
and reversed, here, to backwards.

*

He said: Suppose you'd loved someone and you
wrote out of that. Suppose that. A boy staring out of
the window into the night, figures moving casually in
the street below. A radio on in the darkened and humid
room, intense music.

This is an attempted destruction of my own
beginnings.

*

I walked to the top of a terraced park to meet them;
but at midnight we found ourselves at a café, lost, the
poorly lit streets all alike. In the heat people lay down
to sleep on the pavement or on top of parked cars.
Through large square gaps left in the pavement we
could see the sewers; someone told me of a man who
fell down one of these holes during a storm and was
found in a river across the other side of the city, dead.

The woman (impeccable voice, impeccable manners, English, upper middle-class), said to me, Look at the cat, (a skinny cat, obviously underfed), why don't they feed it? The answer should have been self-evident. She wrote to thank me for my writing, saying it was wisdom. I am not that man. I am not that man, so, midnight, we found ourselves at a café, lost, the streets all alike. In the heat people lay down to sleep on the pavement. Some of them were not sleeping. They were sick, or decrepit; they couldn't get up.

*

Gérard dreamt that he had been transported to the Rhine—the place where his father and mother were during the first years of his life and, further, where his mother died. "It appeared to me that I was entering a house I knew well, belonging to one of my mother's uncles, a Flemish painter who had been dead more than a century." Clock-time was here destroyed: people of various times all being alive together. (Compare the sonnet 'Artemis': the thirteenth, the number outside (clock-) time, or the beginning of the new cycle (the first number after the twelfth, the twelfth hour), brings back "the only one" and "the only moment". To the

Christian saints Nerval opposed the goddess Artemis who, he said, had always loved him: to her falls the role of *rescuer,* and as such she is Isis, and Aurélia.) A bird which Gerard believed to be inhabited by his grandfather's soul, said to him enigmatically: 'You see your uncle took care to paint *her* portrait in advance.... Now she is with us.' I have the impression that it is Aurélia referred to, painted by the uncle "in advance" of her death; yet when Nerval turned to the portrait he said merely that it was of a woman in "an old German costume", "leaning over a river bank, her eyes fixed on a cluster of forget-me-nots." In the paean of salvation, addressed to Christ, Mary, and Aurélia, Nerval wrote twice (with little variation): "On the crest of a bluish mountain a little flower is born. Forget-me-not. The glittering gaze of a star (the star of his destiny) plays on it for an instant, and an answer is heard in a soft foreign tongue. *Myosotis.*" The forget-me-not (*myosotis*) has an obvious significance, of remembrance and faithfulness (a theme played upon in the second stanza of 'Artemis'). But if the portrayed woman is really Aurélia, then why should she be dressed in an old German costume? I don't know, except for the indirect link with the death of Nerval's own mother in Germany; with his own infatuation with German literature (and it was from

Germany that Nerval first wrote letters of love to Aurélia, "full of German mysticism", as related in *Sylvie*); and especially, it helps link Aurélia with the beloved *Faust* of Goethe, and with the character of Marguerite, whose name has already been invoked in connection with the servant-woman in this dream.

Nerval felt that he had fallen into "a chasm that crossed the world", and was being carried (painlessly) along a stream of molten metal; he saw that the world is criss-crossed with such currents, "like those blood-vessels and veins that writhe in the lobes of the brain". This seems like an image for consciousness itself, with its interrelating strands of thought, memory, emotion, etc. More, a particular *type* (or *part*) of consciousness is being signified, for the "molten metal" has a peculiar significance; and the place to which he was carried existed in a "sunless day"—Nerval remarked elsewhere that one never sees the sun in the world of dreams. Nerval was met by his grandfather, who took him into a house inhabited by various ancestors, including his uncle Antoine Boucher, whom he not only felt close to, but appeared to, almost, identify with. (See *Aurélia* Part Two, IV.) What is localised here is a type of spirit-world, inhabited by the accumulation of past *forms of life* inherited through family, learning, nation, personal choice of life. This was summarised by the uncle when he said: 'We live in our race and our race lives in us.'

*

Adoniram was an artist/craftsman—sculptor, architect and metallurgist—who came upon his knowledge and inspiration in a cavern full of the works of an ancient and mysterious civilisation (—just as Nerval was the "explorer" of Cabalism and the ancient mysteries). Opposed to him was Solomon, aging ruler, poet and thinker, dedicated to the service of Jehovah, to whose glory (or perhaps Solomon's own) the temples on which Adoniram had been hired to work were being built. Both men fell in love with Bilkis, the Queen of Sheba, and she fell in love with, not the ruler Solomon, but Adoniram. Like nearly all the stories that Nerval told, whether his own or others', this ended in tragedy.

The most important part of the story is that involving a descent to the centre of the earth by Adoniram, led by the ghost of Tubal-Cain, who tells him: 'Your feet are standing upon the great emerald which is a root and a pivot for the mountain of Kaf; you have reached the realm of your fathers. Here in undisputed power reigns the lineage of Cain. Beneath these granite fortresses, amid inaccesible caverns, we found liberty at last. Here the jealous tyranny of Adonai (Jehovah) has no more power; here man can eat of the fruit of the Tree of Knowledge and live.' (Tubal-Cain is one of the descendents of Cain, and "an instructor of every artificer in brass and iron", *Genesis*, 4.22. The "great emerald" is possibly a reference to the *Emerald Tablet* of Alchemy; in certain so-called primitive beliefs the emerald is also associated with the solar deity.) As Gérard descended or rather as he says *fell* into a "chasm that crossed the world", and was met by his grandfather, who was in his own way an outcast (he was responsible for a horse being lost from Nerval's great-grandfather's farm, and left the farm in shame), and by his uncle, who was at one time a student of Cabalism and other esoteric doctrines, so Adoniram descended to an "underworld" and found himself with his own "race"—that of the arch-rebel Cain. Nerval seemed at one time to have identified himself with rebels and to have held a dislike of Jehovah—though the God of the Druze, with whom Nerval apparently felt more at home, is much like the Hebrew Jehovah; perhaps it was more the openly evident division between the *wise* and the *ignorant* in relation to "the mysteries", that was so attractive to Nerval, at a particular stage in his life, in the Druze religion. While saying that Jehovah is only *one* of the Elohim (gods), Nerval failed to say who or what the others are; at any rate, he would seem to be a god of balance, as he is opposed to the energy (fire) of Cain's race which is even said to keep the "spark of life" which animates beings. A magic.

*

In another dream-vision, Gérard found himself in a wonderful city high up above our own: "A blessed race had made for itself this retreat beloved of birds, flowers, of pure air and sunlight." Nerval later referred to this place as The Mysterious City. The beauty and compassion of the people there "inspired a sort of love without preference and devoid of all desire, an epitome of all the intoxications of the vague passions of youth." A friend who had later made Nerval tell of these dreams in detail, asked with tears in his eyes: 'Is there a God?' To which Nerval replied enthusiastically: 'Yes!' This comes in *Aurélia* as an intimation (a foreknowledge or preview) of a blessed state which shines, as the oft-mentioned star (the signification of which *turns* or is redeemed in order to, itself, signify redemption), shines over the scenes of spiritual warfare which are to come. It brings to mind, to some extent, what the Consul in Malcolm Lowry's *Under the Volcano* refers to as the path to heaven running straight through hell.

Gérard felt confirmed in a belief in the immortality of the soul ("Another dream of mine confirmed me in this belief", he stated explicitly), by a dream in which, in a place of supernaturally brilliant light, he was in the company of three beautiful women who stood for "relatives and friends of (his) youth. Each seemed to have the features of several of them. Their facial contours changed like the flames of a lamp, and all the time something of one was passing to the other. Their smiles, the colour of their eyes and hair, their figures and familiar gestures, all these were exchanged as if they had lived the same life, and each was made up of all three, like those figures painters take from a number of models in order to achieve a perfect beauty." So too was Nerval's own method of re-creation, in art and life, of the people and the events he loved and was obsessed by. The girls of his childhood—Fanchette, Sylvie, Adrienne—were in a sense one and the same; each participated in the spell of the particular *form of life* which it was Nerval's destiny to be bound to. And just as one of these could become, and was, the other, one ("the eldest") became more definitely Adrienne, the nun who had died (see the end of *Sylvie*), in her disappearance as in her appearance a prefiguration of Aurélia. She pointed out to him that he was now wearing a strange suit which they had made—described as having the textural consistency of a spider-web (the web perhaps being an image of the spell in which he is caught). Whether given to him or just appearing there, it *was* supposedly of their making; and it was like a claim on his being, and an acceptance—a belonging-to. He was, he tells us, charmed by it.

One of these women—I presume it is the same one, as she alone could metamorphose as easily, even in a dream, into Aurélia—went into a neglected garden; Nerval, the gentle pursuer, followed her. In the garden was "a spring of fresh water whose splashes echoed melodiously over a pool of still water, half-hidden by huge water-lilies." As Ross Chambers in his notes on *Sylvie* has pointed out, fresh water was for Nerval symbolic of both life and change; and still water was suggestive of both the stillness of eternity, and death (stagnancy). The woman slid her arm along the stem of a hollyhock (cf. 'Artemis') before she "grew" and dematerialised (though it had already been quite evident she was chimerical), until her form blended with the garden and the sky. It was a death that was revealed, meaning loss for Gérard, who in anguish declared that the earth for him was now bereft of its animating spirit, who had merged completely with the *form* of the spirit-world:

> *I lost her thus as she became transfigured, for she seemed to vanish in her own immensity.*
>
> *'Don't leave me!' I cried. 'For with you Nature itself dies.' With these words I struggled painfully through the brambles trying to grasp the vast shadow that eluded me. I threw myself on a fragment of ruined wall, at the foot of which lay the marble bust of a woman. I lifted it up and felt convinced it was of her... I recognised the beloved features and as I stared around me I saw that the garden had become a graveyard, and I heard voices crying: 'The universe is in darkness'.*

The garden a graveyard; like the loss of paradise. After having informed us that it was only much later that he learned of Aurélia's death, Gèrard mentioned a ring he had given to her, but as it was too large, had conceived the "fatal" idea of having it cut down: as the saw cut into it, he seemed to see blood coming from it (a detail Geoffrey Wagner suggests is derived from a story of Hoffmann's about a Cabalist). He also thought of how, when they were *both* dead, they could be together again—a selfish thought, as he admitted, costing "bitter remorse".

*

It was after he learned of Jenny Colon's death that Gérard set off for the Middle East.

*

At Damietta, in a forest whose trees "look like so many columns in a temple dedicated to universal nature", Nerval reflected upon his age: "...for a few months (in the Orient) I have felt myself going back again upon the circle of my days. I feel younger, and in truth I am younger; I am only twenty years old." The forest was fenced by water on one side and desert on the other; the suggestions in some respects of the landscapes of *Sylvie*, so strangely re-encountered, brought him back to his youth; and again he found someone who, like Adrienne or Aurélia (both dead), became his ideal. "The ideal woman whom every man pursues in his dreams had realised herself for me: the rest was all forgotten." The girl was a young and beautiful Druze maiden named

Salema. "Fate or Providence, we sometimes seem to see, appears beneath the drab monotony of life, a line drawn upon some mysterious pattern, which points the way which we must follow, or go astray. I immediately came to the conclusion that it had been written from all time that I should marry in Syria; that Fate had so far foreseen this tremendous fact, that for its realisation nothing less was needed than a thousand circumstances strangely interwoven in my existence, whose relationship to one another I doubtless exaggerated."

Nerval found himself in a position to aid Salema's father; he hoped that the Druze sheik might look favourably, because of this, on a marriage. But while musing on his destiny and his love, Nerval had before been surprised by an ill augury: "I hardly dare tell you what a very ordinary event brought me to earth again, as I was spurning the red sand with a proud foot. An enormous insect crossed my path, pushing before it a ball greater than itself; it was a kind of beetle, and reminded me of the Egyptian scarabs which carry the world upon their heads. You know I am superstitious, and you may well imagine that I drew an augury from this symbolic intervention across my path. I retraced my steps, convinced there must be some obstacle against which I should have to fight."

The Druze religion, founded by Hamza ibn Ali and Fatimid caliph Al-Hakim, at the beginning of the 11th century AD, is a form of syncretic religious faith, rather like the modem Persian "world-faith" Baha'i, and resembling it also in that it is often regarded as an Islamic heresy by Muslims. "Let us", said Nerval, "say that the beliefs of the Druses are a synthesis of all the religions and philosophies that have gone before." The divine truths are successively revealed to mankind, which would otherwise always exist in "darkness", through the "stations" of the Prophets (relating to the "manifestations" of God). (According to the Baha'is, the last and highest was their founder, Baha'u'llah; for the Muslims the "seal" of the law was Muhammed, and this explains, at least in part, why they are so hostile to Baha'is. Muslim hostility to the Druze is not something to try to go into here.)

For Nerval, who wished to pursue a synthesis of religions, the Druze religion no doubt looked to be what he had been searching for. And assuming that all religions are looked upon equally, more or less, by the Druze, he approached the father of Salema, asking for her hand. However, it was revealed to him soon enough that the sheik's people alone are considered "the elect of God"; and when Al-Hakim returns from the dead (the spirit-world, heaven, or whatever), the Druze will have power over the earth and the rest of humanity will be their slaves. One can, of course, recognise here the desire for power rather than the desire for religious salvation; and the twin ideas of "the elect people" and Messianism: at least in as far as Nerval's account goes.

Gérard tried to persuade the sheik—and himself—that he (Gérard) may have been descended from a Druze convert, by firstly attempting to tie up the Druze religion with Freemasonry and Rosicrucianism through the Knights Templar in the Lebanon, and then by producing a Freemason's diploma, "full of cabalistic signs familiar to the Orientals". The sheik was (surprisingly) convinced, and Nerval became both Salema's fiancé and a student of the esoteric "mysteries" of the Druze faith, involving "nine stages of initiation", and hidden from the "ignorant" amongst the faithful. But Nerval found that the climate of the Lebanon endangered his health, and he was forced to leave his ideal woman and the mysteries of the Druze, and go to Constantinople.

*

Nerval attempted while in the asylum to write a mythical "world-history" influenced, as he said, by Oriental traditions. In the beginning, so his account goes, the seven Elohim inhabited the world together peacefully. "But one of the Elohim conceived the idea of creating a fifth race composed of earthly elements and to be called *Afrites*. This was the signal for a complete revolution among the Spirits who did not wish to recognise these new lords of the world." There seems to be a confusion in this, unconscious or wilful. *Afrites* are evil spirits; yet the refusal to recognise a "race composed of earthly elements" sounds like the refusal of Lucifer in the Bible, and Eblis (Serpent or Devil) in the Koran, to recognise Adam (man). Or, perhaps the refusal to be man as the servant of Jehovah (like Abel) and not man who follows Eblis and rebels against Jehovah (as Cain does). In outlining the Druze theory of history in *Voyage en Orient* Nerval mentions Eblis:

(Besides the Prophets) there necessarily exists, also, angels of darkness who play the opposite part (i.e. of bondage and destruction instead of salvation).

So in the history of the world, according to the Druses, we find each of the seven periods the scene of tremendous action, when in human form these enemies seek out one another and are to be recognised by their greatness or their hatred.

So, in turn, the spirit of evil is Eblis, or the serpent; Methouzael, king of the city of the giants, at the period of the Flood; Nimrod, at the time of Abraham; Pharoah, at the time of Moses; and later, Antiochus, Herod, and other monstrous tyrants, assisted by sinister acolytes, who are reborn at the same periods, to fight against the reign of the Lord.

And this could be substituted, almost *en bloc,* for the account which appears in *Aurélia.* Three Elohim are banished "to the ends of the earth", taking with them "powerful Cabalists" who would seem to take the place of the "sinister acolytes" in *Voyage en Orient.* These Elohim dominate a section of the human race, and the sufferings of the people under their reign leaves no doubt of its evil. Nerval too was under the weight of it: "for a long time I groaned there in captivity...."

There is both ambivalence and ambiguity throughout this account, as should become obvious in the following.

The three Elohim and their Cabalistic helpers are

banished; in the same way as the "race of Cain", who keep the fire which is, amongst other things, the "fire" of genius, the "god-like" inspiration and imagination of the artist, who is rebel and outcast in the Romantic scheme of things. Eblis was said to be the only angel who refused to obey God's order to worship Adam, on the grounds that Adam had been made of clay and he had been made of fire. In his Eastern notebooks Nerval described himself as "one of the *widow's* (Isis') *children*, a young wolf (a master's son), brought up in horror of the murder of Adoniram and in admiration of the holy Temple...." It is clear from *Voyage* that, at that time, Nerval identified himself with Adoniram, the artist, smith (guardian of fire), rebel and member of the race of Cain. Eblis—fire—Cain (through Tubal-Cain); there are definite and enlightening links there: "In the 2nd century AD there was a Gnostic sect who perversely maintained that Cain was the offspring of Eve by a superior power, while Abel was her son by an inferior power; that his slaying of Abel was symbolic of the victory of superior over inferior power; and that he became the ancestor of Esau, Judas Iscariot, and other generally reprobated characters." (E R Pike.)

The domination is brought to an end by the Flood; "for forty days a mysterious ark floated on the waters, bearing the hope of a new creation". And while Nerval, who believed in a naive variety of reincarnation, can be said to be on one level setting out a "world-history" in which, as he states, he participates from the beginning, on the symbolical plane we can see analogies with his spiritual life. The words "new creation" bring to mind many associations: re-creation; new life; new consciousness; new world.

The Elohim are seven in number; three of them turn against the other four:

> All through remote Asiatic and African civilisations a bloody scene of orgy and carnage was constantly renewed, reproduced by the same spirits under different forms.
>
> The last one took place at Granada, where the sacred talisman fell before the hostile blows of Christians and Moors. How many more years yet has the world still to suffer, for the vengeance of those eternal enemies must inevitably be renewed under other skies! They are the severed sections of the serpent that encircles the Earth... separated by steel, they join together again in a hideous embrace cemented by human blood.

It is the forces of domination and will-to-power which could be identified with the three Elohim.

Religious intolerance is, as one thing amongst many, implicated in this; we know from the end of *Voyage en Orient* that Gérard firmly believed in religious tolerance.

Near the beginning of the legend, Nerval wrote: "Only the pale light of the stars lit the bluing perspectives of this strange horizon; yet, as the work of creation proceeded, a brighter star began to draw from it the germs of its own future brilliance." Then later: "A radiant goddess guided the speedy evolution of man through... *new metamorphoses*." The "radiant goddess" draws harmony from chaos; but when the Elohim, and their attendant spirits and sorcerers, begin fighting, and the Deluge comes: "... I can still see a woman standing on a peak lapped by the waters they abandoned, crying out with dishevelled hair and struggling against death. Her pitiful cries rose above the noise of the waters.... Was she saved? I do not know. Her brothers, the gods, had condemned her; but over her shone the Evening Star throwing its flaming rays upon her forehead." And preceding the passage beginning, "All through remote Asiatic and African civilisations": "Everywhere the suffering image of the eternal Mother was dying, weeping, or languishing." The Evening Star is usually Venus, and so could carry here the associations of the goddess of that planet. Venus was for Nerval Isis and the Virgin both (he tells us that in Greece he found the cult of Venus carried on in the name of the Virgin by the peasants), a Venus "austere, ideal and mystic", turning one's mind away from "impure thoughts". Thus the abandoned woman could be seen as Venus "abandoned" due to forces of strife. In his struggle with the friend who "took on the aspect of an Apostle", Nerval cried, 'I don't belong to your Heaven. Those in that star are waiting for me. Let me go to them, for the one I love belongs to them, and it is there we are to meet again.' And in 'El Desdichado' he wrote of Aurélia: "My sole *star* is dead".

*

Despite the disturbing quality of some of his dreams and hallucinations, Nerval spoke of the asylum as "a paradise" for him, which he left when calm had returned. Long afterwards, an accident caused a relapse which brought a continuation of the "series of dreams". Nerval, walking in the country, saw a bird which reminded him of the dream bird which was supposed to house his grandfather's spirit; but it gave him "a foreboding of evil". Immediately after the encounter with the bird, he met a friend who asked him to look over his estate; ". . . in the course of doing so he made me climb a raised terrace with him, from which could be seen a wide view. It was sunset. As we descended the steps of a rustic stair I stumbled and struck my chest against the angle of a piece of garden furniture. I had just enough strength left to get up and dash into the middle of the garden, thinking I had received a death blow and wanting, before I died, to cast a last glance at the setting sun. Through all the regrets that such a moment brings, I felt happy to be dying in this way, at this hour, surrounded by the trees, trellises and autumn flowers." However, he soon recovered from the swoon sufficiently to go home, but there had an attack of fever. Thinking of the view from his friend's terrace he remembered a cemetery which was the very one Aurélia was buried in. Approaching death—the bird—the climbing—the garden with its flowers and trellises—Aurélia's death: this seems like a recapitulation of much that has come before. When Gerard was in the Mysterious City, "a man, dressed in white, whose face I was not able to see clearly, threatened me with a weapon he held in his hand: but my guide signed to him to go away. It appeared as though they had wished to stop me from penetrating the mysteries of these retreats." Now this man *had* struck him, and the blow was that which he received when he fell on the stairs. Gérard, in his studies of Cabalistic magic, had apparently tried to force an entrance, through what Geoffrey Wagner calls "an excess of intellectual curiosity", into realms where he had not the right to enter. In his sleep, it seemed "that a whole fatal race had been let loose in that ideal world I had previously seen, and of which (Aurélia) was the queen. The same Spirit who had threatened me when I entered the dwelling of those pure families who lived in the *Mysterious City* passed before me, no longer in the white robes he had worn then, together with the rest of his race, but dressed like an Oriental prince. I rushed towards him, threateningly, but he turned calmly and— to my terror and fury—it was my own face, my whole form magnified and idealised.... Then I remembered the man who had been arrested on the same night as myself and whom, as I thought, the guard had released under my name when my two friends came to fetch me. In his hand he held some weapon the shape of which I could not properly see, and one of those with him said: 'That was what he struck him with.' "

In *Voyage en Orient* Nerval had told the legend of the Caliph Hakem (Al-Hakim) of Cairo. Hakem pronounced himself God—for which he has been regarded by the Muslims as a fanatic or a madman. Two things in particular in Nerval's version of Hakem's story link up with the above: first, Hakem at one point is thrown into an asylum, and when the minister of affairs visits the madhouse, Hakem cries at him: "Wretch!... have you then created a phantom to resemble me and take my place?"; second, the Caliph prepares to marry his beautiful sister Setalmulc, whom he believes to have been destined to be his "from all time", but the night before the wedding, as he comes back to the palace he finds a feast underway. "He felt that he had passed to the condition of a shade, an invisible spirit, and went on from room to room, passing through the groups as though he had worn upon his finger the magic ring of Gyges." (The ring of Gyges bestowed invisibility upon its wearer.) Hakem sees his double seated beside his sister Setalmulc: "He realised that this was his *ferouer,* or double, and for an Oriental to see his own spectre is a sign of the most foreboding augury. The shade compels the body to follow it before the next day is done." "Was not this some jealous divinity, seeking to usurp his place in Heaven by taking Setalmulc from her brother, separating a couple which Providence had itself ordained? Was this the race of *dives,* by such means trying to substitute its own most impious progeny?"

The whole thing turns out to be not at all as ghostly

as it sounds in this fragment—only some of the links between persons and events seem "weird". It is actually Setalmulc who plots against her brother, and even has him set upon by assassins. But isn't this rather understandable, anyway?—The Caliph ignores all laws of moderation; he proclaims himself God, thus *absolute* ruler and *sole* authority; he attempts an incestuous marriage with his sister.

One of the twin spirits in a man, Gérard suggested, is evil, the other good. If nothing else, he knew the "other" was hostile to him. And the other, the *ferouer,* had taken Gérard's place to marry Aurélia in his stead. "Well, I told myself, I must fight against this spirit of destiny, *fight even against God himself* with the weapons of tradition and science."

In the next dream Gérard came first to a workshop where animals and flowers were made, animated by fire which, so he was told, "animated the first living creatures". These passages are strongly reminiscent of the workshop of Tubal-Cain, where precious stones and minerals were produced: '...we prepare the metals, and distribute them in the veins of the planet, after we have liquefied their vapours.' Fire is an important symbol in Nerval—multi-suggestive: of emotional warmth; sexual passion; genius; divinity. Fire has been a symbol for life—for example, for the Parsees. The Greek Hephaestus, equivalent of the Roman Vulcan, the divine smith and god of fire, was, although born of Zeus and Hera (King and Queen of Heaven), an outcast from heaven to earth, and the husband of Aphrodite. He also made the first woman, Pandora, whose name Nerval used in one of his stories. I am noting all these things, because metallurgy traditionally has sinister symbolic connotations.

Being connected with alchemy, and hence with astrology and human destiny (the metals are linked with the planets), metallurgy has been considered, according to its employment, beneficent *or* maleficent. René Guénon writes in *The Reign of Quantity* that the increasing use of metals in our time is likely "a symptom of a more 'advanced' phase in the downward movement of the cycle (of the presumed "Dark Age"); and this supposition is confirmed by the fact that in a general way metal plays an ever-growing part in the 'industrialised' and 'mechanised' civilisation of today; and that from a destructive point of view, if it may be so expressed, no less than from a constructive point of view, for the consumption of metal brought about by modern wars is truly prodigious". Guénon associates Tubal-Cain with Vulcan, and remarks significantly: "...

and it must not be forgotten that from the traditional point of view metals and metallurgy are in direct relation with the 'subterranean fire', the idea of which is associated in many respects with that of the 'infernal regions'." Frithjof Schuon is also of this opinion (*Spiritual Perspectives and Human Facts*): "In a certain, external, sense it may be said that the great social and political evil of the West is mechanisation, for it is the machine which most directly engenders the great evils from which the world today is suffering. The machine is, generally speaking, characterised by *the use of iron, of fire and of invisible forces*. To talk about a wise use of machines, of their serving the human spirit, is utterly chimerical. It is in the very nature of mechanisation to reduce men to slavery and to devour them entirely, leaving them nothing human, nothing above the animal level, nothing above the collective level. The kingdom of the machine followed that of iron, or rather gave to it its most sinister expression. Man, who created the machine, ends by becoming its creature." (My italics)

If Nerval's Hakem is an ambivalent figure (for example, he preaches universal religious tolerance, yet early in the story exclaims, "Mohammed and Jesus are impostors" in a most vehement fashion), we know that Nerval approved of him, and to some degree identified with him—yet probably more so with the Sabaean boatman, Yousouf, also in love with Hakem's sister Setalmulc (the name, incidentally, means The Lady of the Kingdom). Hakem's delusions of being God, and Yousouf's visions of Setalmulc, are realised under the influence of hashish, as Nerval's delusions of grandeur, and visions of Aurélia, were realised during his madness—which at times he spoke of apologetically to the reader, at other times praised. Yousouf himself is made to say: "Sometimes I am near to thinking that it is all an illusion caused by this treacherous weed, which is perhaps attacking my reason... so that I can no longer distinguish between dream and reality." Gérard came to view his interpretations as false; but in *Voyage* he vindicated both Hakem and Yousouf. Hakem's *ferouer* is Yousouf—two halves of a single reality, as it were: magus and platonic lover. Or Gérard de Nerval. But if in the legend of Hakem it is the double of "God" who is to marry in the other's stead, in *Aurélia* it is God who was to marry in Gérard's stead.

After coming from the workshop, in *Aurélia*, Nerval found himself in the midst of a crowd assembled for wedding festivities. Imagining this wedding to be that of his double with Aurélia, Nerval began to make a commotion, pleading his case to those he knew amongst the gathering. He shouted that he was not afraid of the *doppelgänger* because he knew the sign with which to defeat him. One of the men from the workshop appeared, and threatened him with a red-hot ball at the end of a metal bar. His own world—the world of Adoniram—seemed to have turned against him, that is, assisting in his "downfall". "Everyone around me seemed to be jeering at my impotence.... I stepped back to the throne then, my soul filled with unutterable pride, and raised my arm to make a sign which to me appeared to have magical power. A woman's cry, vibrant and clear, and filled with excruciating agony, woke me with a start. The syllables of the unknown word I had been about to utter died on my lips.... I threw myself on the floor and began praying fervently, weeping warm tears." This voice, though he was convinced it came from the "real world", he was as thoroughly convinced was in some unexplainable way Aurélia's.

"What had I done? I had disturbed the harmony of the magic universe, from which my soul drew the certainty of immortal existence. Perhaps I was cursed for having offended divine law by wishing to penetrate a terrible mystery. I could only expect anger and scorn! The furious shadows fled shrieking, describing fatal circles in the air, like birds before the approach of a storm."

The sonnet 'El Desdichado', perhaps the most extraordinary of the sequence *Les Chimères* (*Chimeras*), provides what is practically an *index* to Nerval's work. The title means 'The Disinherited', or as Brian Hill renders it, 'Fortune's Fool'. In the poem, Nerval compares himself to Orpheus, the poet/musician whose wife Eurydice had died: Orpheus went down into hell, as Nerval considered himself to have done, and was allowed to bring her up from the underworld, on condition that on the ascent he didn't look back at her; this he did, however, and she was again lost to him. After his defiance of the guardians of the spirit-world in Part One of *Aurélia,* Nerval employs the words "Eurydice! Eurydice!" as a motto for Part Two, the very first words of which are "Lost once more!"

'El Desdichado' concerns a loss: the death of Isis' embodiment, Aurélia, and the distance now between Gérard and Isis, the Ideal. He is the man consigned to darkness, to the realm of shadows; the descendant of a knight (so he believed) of the Aquitaine, whose tower is in ruins—the ruined tower, according to S A Rhodes, being a Cabalistic symbol designating exclusion "from the earthly paradise as a divine punishment". The guiding star of his destiny is gone; his fate, from birth. (The lines "my constellated lute/ Bears the black *sun* of *Melancholia*", refers on the first hand to the designation of *lute* in Gui Le Fèvre de La Broderie's *Les trois livres de la vie de M Ficin* as the human physiognomy as its own genethliacal index (information researched by Jean Richer); second, to Dürer's etching of the Angel of Melancholia with the black sun of misfortune—an engraving which Nerval makes reference to in Part One of *Aurélia*. The darkness in which he now resides is a "grave", and he begs the one who has consoled him (presumably Isis) to give back those images of his loves: the Posilipo hills and the Italian sea (the visit to Italy, where he met the English girl Octavie in the story of that name), "the *flower* so dear to (his) tormented heart" (the "Mauve-hearted rose, flower of Saint Gudule" ('Artemis'); Nerval went to Brussels in 1840 to see a revival of his play *Piquillo,* starring Jenny Colon, and spent much time in a "church of miracles"—that of Saint Gudule), and the "grape-vines enlaced among the roses" at Sylvie's window. He asks, "Am I Amor or Phoebus? ... Lusignan or Biron?", that is, is he Love (the lover) or the artist who makes art in love's honour (Phoebus is the god of light and of poetry; and in the temple of Isis at Pompeii

Nerval found that the main statue bore an inscription at the base "saying that L C Phoebus had erected it there by decree of the decurions"); has he been the lover of a nymph or of a real woman (Lusignan was the husband of a mermaid, losing her when he discovered her secret, having disobeyed her instructions; Biron has been given a few identifications, but that of John W Kneller, "the celebrated Perigordian hero Biron" who unlike Lusignan was a successful lover, seems appropriate). His answer is that his forehead is still marked with the kiss of Adrienne in childhood, and that in the sea-cave where Venus was born (and which he saw when in Greece) and where the siren swims, he has had a dream—the dream of his love, his life, and the dreams that take over his life when he becomes mad—for indeed more than once has he crossed over the river of death (or insanity), the Acheron, in search of his beloved, in his dreams seeing her, and come back again, having on the lyre of Orpheus played the cries of his pagan love (epitomised by the story *Sylvie*) and the "sighs of a saint" (Adrienne-as-nun), the two sides of Nerval's own nature.

A decisive event was his visit to a sick friend, who talked to him of the inner spirit of a man, which manifests God; this inner spirit, this Christ-principle of the soul, was with Nerval's friend, so Gérard was led to believe—but not with himself: "Oh, misery, I have driven Him from me, I have threatened Him, I have cursed Him! It was indeed He, the mystic brother, Who drifted further and further from my soul and warned me in vain. The Beloved Bridegroom, King of Glory, it is He who has judged and condemned me, and taken to His own Heaven the woman He gave me and of whom I am now unworthy for ever!" So the Double, who was formerly "an evil genius", had become the "King of Glory".

While engaged in exploring the Pyramid of Cheops (*Voyage*), Nerval had met a German traveller who told him of initiation rites in the Cult of Isis. The latter part of this account (following a description of more physically-based trials) is of especial interest:

...*he was put through an examination (by the Cult's*

priests) in which all the actions of his life were analysed and criticised. This lasted for another twelve days; then he was made to sleep for nine more days behind the statue of Isis, after which he had implored the goddess to appear to him and inspire him with wisdom in his dreams. At last, after about three months, the trials were completed. The neophyte's aspiration towards divinity, encouraged by his reading, instruction and fasting, aroused in him such a pitch of religious enthusiasm that he was at last worthy to see the sacred veils of the goddess fall before him. Then, his astonishment reached its height as he saw that cold statue come to life, and its features suddenly take the form of those of the woman he had loved the most, or the ideal which he had formed for himself of the most perfect beauty.

The moment he stretched out his arms to take her, she vanished in a cloud of perfume. The priests entered with great ceremony and the initiate was proclaimed like unto the gods. . . . (The emphasis is mine.)

The adoration of Isis—the *trials* (and Nerval explicitly refers to his sufferings in *Aurélia* as "this series of trials")—the studies in esoteric doctrines—the perusal of the past—the dreams—all these things and more can be pointed to as similarities between the German's account and *Aurélia*.

The German traveller concluded his story by saying that the neophyte is now allowed to live in a Paradise garden; yet as one final test he is forbidden to eat the fruit of a certain tree. This he does, whereupon he is expulsed from the Paradise and goes out into the world to teach others what the priests have taught him. At this point, Nerval said to the Prussian: I think you have been telling me the story of Adam and Eve. If this is the case, then the sin of the initiate is that of *hubris* (likewise the fault of Hölderlin's Empedocles): "(the serpent said:) ye shall be as gods ..." (*Genesis,* 3:5). Or at least: unnatural curiosity.

*

At the onset of the crisis, Nerval's mind converted what was only a rain-storm into the beginning of a flood; significantly, he had been made to think of the Flood by seeing monsters at a Natural History museum. By the Flood the world was purified. Nerval's world-history, climaxed by the Flood, had begun with the advent of monsters; (the Goddess had figured in that story also). But flooding of course is also disaster, and Nerval dispelled it (in his own mind) by throwing a silver ring into the waters. Following this, a goddess appeared to Gérard in a dream, telling him: "I am the same as Mary, the same as your mother, the same being also whom you have always loved under every form. At each of your ordeals I have dropped one of the masks with which 1 hide my features and soon you shall see me as 1 really am." This is reminiscent of the vision of Isis in *The Golden Ass* and, knowing Nerval's preoccupations, one can assume that it is Isis who speaks the words. For Nerval, Venus was Isis, and in *Voyage en Orient* he gave an Orphic fragment revealing something of the goddess' nature: "Venerable goddess who lovest the shades... visible and invisible... from whom all things emanate, for thou givest laws to the whole world and thou commandest even the Fates, O ruler of the Night!" And in *Aurélia* we find: "1 turned my thoughts to the eternal Isis, sacred mother and spouse; all my aspirations, all my prayers were mingled in that magic name, and I seemed to live again in her; sometimes she appeared to me in the guise of Venus of the ancients, sometimes as the Christian Virgin."

In a dream Aurélia herself appeared, after Nerval had been taken by Saturninus from a tower, the tower of his solitary musings, where he had spent all his time climbing up and down staircases; she said: "The ordeal you have undergone is coming to an end; these countless stairways which wore you out so going up and down are the bonds of old illusions that impeded your thoughts; now remember the day when you implored the Holy Virgin and, thinking her dead, were possessed by a frenzy of the mind. Your vow must be carried to her by a simple soul, one free from the ties of the earth. She is near you and that is why I myself have been permitted to come and encourage you."

*

Aurélia had been "sleeping in some palace", some other existence, where Gérard, here, could not reach her.

The image. Upside-down, laughing; the motion of the swing caught. The image caught: laughter in a face, an image catching me transversely; the motion of the swing caught, forwards, and reversed, here, to backwards.

*

It is the Rose Pearl, Gérard said, which resisted the hammer-blow of pride, *hubris* of fire and forge—the hammer-blow which broke the holy table, and attempted to break the world. But Gérard was under the protection of Apollo, god of poetry and of medicine; and like Adonis he was the beloved of Aphrodite.

1971—1978
Melbourne—London

A FINAL WAVE

A FINAL WAVE

I've journeyed here again, along a route I never remember yet always follow, never clear except in the instance, yet always there. It's only a short distance now to the sea, with its waves breaking over rocks, cliffs high above, and only an equally short walk in the other direction to the town, with its arcades, shops, cafés and public houses... and then hills in the distance.

*

In my hotel room: a yellow flower in a glass globe. And caught within the glass: iridescent drops, tiny globules of light.

I arrived late, yet just in time for a meal: cheese and bacon omelette, salad on the side. Not bad at all.

I'm promised waffles for breakfast.

*

Lashing rain has been my lot ever since arriving here. *Flagellating*.

A young woman sits in the branches of a tree. As I approach, she calls out: 'Listen!' So I sit down on the wet grass and listen.

' "I'll catch you!" cried the mother koala, as her joey fell from the bough. "Here", said the bear, scooping the crow out of water festooned with weeds onto the bank and then walking away; the crow was too astonished to say anything. "I'll speak now", exclaimed the stone. And it began its story...'

Suddenly she jumps down, and just as suddenly I lose consciousness. I wake up with a headache and a bump on the head: presumably due to a kick which somehow I never saw.

*

Sheet lightning tonight.

*

'Oh, *her!* She's a crazy one, she is. One of those animal rights activists, and more.'

'Camps out somewhere in the hills. Or so I've heard.'

'She's a fierce one. As well as being strange. *Dead* strange, I'd say.'

I notice a jukebox in a corner of the pub: one of the old-fashioned kind, large and brightly painted, decorated with flashing lights. There are a couple of Randy Newman songs, 'Sail Away' and 'Small People', and I play them both.

When I go the bar, the publican says, 'No one likes that second song you played. It never gets played by any of *us*. We've been meaning to remove it.'

I notice for the first time that he's standing on a little platform behind the bar.

As the great jazz musician Lester Young used to say, *I can feel a draught.*

*

Waves rising, washing, spreading over the rocks at the base of the cliff and the path I'm walking on, wetting my feet despite my shoes. (Why didn't I bring boots? I ask myself.)

When I reach the top, and walk some ways, I'm astonished to suddenly encounter a troop of baboons: what on earth are they doing here? One of them runs up to me and seems inclined to be friendly; I sense no danger and feel no fear, though this changes when some orang-utans pass by, carrying planks of wood and, more worryingly, hammers and saws. The baboons don't seem concerned, so I try to appear indifferent, though my heart's beating fast. Then I remember that I've heard something about an experiment in these parts, called The Barque Project....

*

I enter a pub and there she is! "The wild girl", as I think of her.

I sit down opposite her. 'Murder has been committed here', she says, without the least prompting. And then gets up and leaves.

*

'The cliffs are haunted! No one goes there, apart from the bloody animals. Didn't you see the sign?'

'I saw something that said, EE UT. Afraid I didn't take much notice of it.'

'That was KEEP OUT! Some of the letters have faded away, that's all.'

'We don't go up there', someone else says, 'but the

animals come down here when they think it's safe. Poaching. And stealing! They even steal lumber!'

'Now, that's probably gypsies', says the publican.

'Gypsies, my eye! There haven't been Romanies around here for decades.'

I don't mention that I've seen orang-utans carrying planks. It isn't any business of mine.

'Anyway, when the animals come down from the cliffs, we have a chance to grab them!'

'That's right', another says. 'We caught one of those big ginger-haired apes once—'

'Orang-utans', I say. 'Reddish-brown hair, actually.'

'Whatever! Anyway, we tied it to a pole and threw rotten fruit and vegetables at it, then eggs, then rocks and stones. It was utterly hysterical, right up to the time it died—and we were in hysterics.'

I take my drink to a table of my own in a far corner.

*

To my even greater surprise than before, the wild girl joins me. She'd evidently been sitting in the shadows somewhere in the pub.

'I hate humans', she says viciously. '*And that includes you.*' She finishes her drink, and abruptly leaves.

*

I've been doing a little research.

Orang-utans are possibly the gentlest of the ape family, as well as amongst the most intelligent.

But even if the townsfolk didn't know this, any more than I had, their attitudes and behaviour were disgusting and grotesque.

An emotional numbing? Emotional blindness, so to speak? (Or is this insulting to the blind?) A refusal, conscious or unconscious, to see that we're fellow sentient creatures: able to feel pain and, yes, have feelings? Or a deliberate decision to be cruel, where you can, usually, with animals, rather than where you most often can't, that is, with other people—without fear of redress or retaliation, at any rate?

I remember—from when I was a boy—my mother trying to remonstrate with our next door neighbour, who allowed his son to pluck the feathers from live birds. He seemed to think it amusing that Mum would care.... The cries distressed and haunted me.

A little more research: I find that The Barque Project was founded by a female philanthropist and animal-lover, who recruited occasional help from volunteers to establish a sanctuary where a variety of animals, including carnivores, were raised to co-exist peacefully, both with each other and with the project's workers, and to roam freely along the cliff tops. Some of the animals, such as the orang-utans, were also taught certain skills: in particular, basic carpentry. Just how far the experiment had succeeded and developed is open to speculation. But two things were clear: first, the townsfolk had opposed the project right from the beginning; and second, the founder had mysteriously disappeared, her disappearance surrounded by rumours of foul play, although no proof of this has ever come to light.

*

'Haven't heard that name in quite a long time! She left here some years back.'

I point out that the philanthropist only vanished two years ago, according to the reports I've been reading.

'Ah yes, that's right: I remember now, it was *two* years ago when she left.'

'And she should have taken those bloody animals with her!' someone adds.

*

The weather only gets worse. I'm a fool to venture out at all.

*

At the far end of town: 'We are inbred, it's true!'

'And proud of it! No outsiders will taint *our* gene pool!'

I won't return to that particular pub, either.

*

Up on the cliffs again, I decide to explore further than before. But once I've reached a certain point, I'm met by groups of baboons, orang-utans and gorillas, all blocking my path. They don't try to attack me, but it's clear they do not want me to continue along this way. I turn and go back.

*

Newscasters on TV, computers and radio tell us of travail globe-wide: gales, storms, floods, hurricanes, tsunamis....

'Heavy rain in deserts, even...', someone comments.

*

'Something to do with polar ice caps? Icebergs melting? What a lot of tosh! Icebergs don't bloody well melt. And what if they *did*?'

'If you believe that, you'll believe anything! Bloody so-called ethnic cleansing, for example. Just fucking propaganda!'

'So what's wrong with being clean, anyway?'

'Bloody cry-babies! And then Liberal softies get on the case!'

'Fucking Commies, too! Should all be destroyed, like the scum they are!'

'No, that's not what it's about! There's *nothing real* to it at all. It just never really happens! Smoke and mirrors.'

'Like the Gulf War! Oh, come on! Fucking media rubbish!'

Fortunately there are still a couple of other pubs in this town I can try....

*

Broadcasting has now ceased... or at least, nothing is being received here, not any more; possibly never again? The last I heard was that wherever less threat and actual harm prevailed, borders quickly closed. Fear, selfishness and enmity, long abroad in some places, submerged or incipient in others, have waxed or erupted.

*

We've been hit by cyclones as well as storms, and the damage and danger increases daily.

The more torrential the rains, the more the waters rise: *obviously*. Buildings have been evacuated, with more and more people moving to the hills: rowboats and dinghies being mobilised.

The cliffs are still considered out of bounds. Haunted, as they say. *But why?* Was the philanthropist killed there? The body would have to have been dismembered and the remains hidden under rocks.

Would the townsfolk really have resorted to this?

Having gathered what food and drink I can, and bought myself a tent and a dinghy, I'm abandoning the town while it's still possible. However, I doubt that the hills will be safe for much longer. Accordingly I'll take to the cliffs.

*

Struck by lightning, waves, terrible winds—the buildings are collapsing. The sea has broken through barriers; sandbags have proved of little or no help. Landslides are destroying the hills, and the earth tipped into the sea has caused the water to rise further and further. Screams, prayers, curses are heard as buildings turn to rubble and hills crumble, and people are swept into the waves and out to sea.

*

The wild girl suddenly appears and punches me hard in the face, knocking me to the ground. I get to my feet and in my anger retaliate: I kick her in the ribs and she goes down. Feeling ashamed, I try to help her up but she hits out at me. I'm sorry to say I kick her again. She lies there unconscious.

The baboons chatter, and then shake their heads, as do the orang-utans. And then they wave goodbye.

It hits me now: *this* ark is not going to include any humans at all.

A dove flies over. I look up just as it shits.

*

They've left: walked off into the distance. I've followed, as stealthily as possible. And I can now see what I was never allowed to see before. I'm taken aback by the sheer array of animals—far more diverse and numerous than I'd supposed—and by the size of their vessel. How long did it take them to build it, for God's sake?

Though I don't really think they will notice, I wave back to them as they disappear into the Barque.

DARWIN:
MY TIME
ON THE
LEFT BANK

Call me Darwin. Everyone does.

How did I come to be in Paris? And why in those heady days?

I made my way from Africa, I'd rather not say *where* in Africa, not *exactly*, you understand. Why not? you ask. Ah, well... There are always reasons, no?

But *when* is more important. To my story, that is.

I remember it very well indeed.

I admit I'd been in the Congo for some time. I won't say what I'd been doing there.

From there I made my way to... does it really matter? I ended up in Paris. And it was the summer of... well, let's just say in the 1940s.

Summer! In Paris!

Ah, you understand, I'm sure....

Somehow I made my way to a small café on what's

known as the Left Bank. I'd heard it was where intellectuals gathered, so I guessed it was the right place for me.

I ordered a banana daiquiri. Delicious. I'd heard about this drink when I was in the Congo, but had never tasted it before.

My appearance seemed a little disturbing, but I was used to that.

There was some hubbub around a rather stout man with spectacles and a pipe. He was writing something, and should have been left alone to do so, I would have said, but all these people were there with him. Talking. Or in some instances just nodding, or looking at him admiringly.

I went over to see if I could help.

The others hushed and moved away. He seemed a little disconcerted, but I looked him straight in the eyes and said:

"What's the problem, my friend?"

"Ah", he said, recovering himself, "I'm writing this philosophical novel, and I'm not sure if the title is quite right, you understand?"

"Tell me", I said.

"I'm thinking it might be called 'Zinc in the Soul', or possibly 'Manganese in the Soul'? Or perhaps 'Aluminium in the Soul'? Ah, I really don't know!"

I took a sip of my banana daiquiri and thought about it for a little while.

"Why not 'Iron in the Soul'?" I said.

"Ah! Magnificent! You are a genius, my dear friend!"

His followers lost their shyness and moved closer.

A couple of the women moved very close indeed.

I'd been accepted.

Accepted... ah, yes. So from that day on I had my regular table at Les Deux Magots. I took to smoking a pipe like my new friend. But I stuck to banana daiquiris and didn't drink beer or wine.

"Dear Darwin", my bespectacled, stout and pipe-smoking friend said to me one day, "I'm thinking of calling this series of novels... one of which is now of course 'Iron in the Soul', thanks to you... 'Paths by Which One Might Eventually Escape'. What do you think?"

I took a sip of my drink and a puff on my pipe. All eyes were on me, including those of some admiring females.

"Hmm, a little wordy, perhaps?"

A shocked hush ensued.

Finally:

"Ah, my friend, then what would *you* suggest?"

"Why not 'The Roads to Freedom?'"

Gasps and coughs and even sneers.

"No, no, he's right!"

"AHHH!" they cried as if one. And some of the women moved even closer. Indeed, one was sitting in my lap, to the annoyance of the others. But I didn't mind. I just took another puff and another sip.

I was *thoroughly* accepted.

Those were indeed heady days.

I had affairs. No point denying it. Jeanne, a film star, and Juliet, a famous singer. They sometimes quarrelled about me, but on the whole we all got along.

"Darwin", they'd coo, "you are so virile, and so strong, and so hairy!" I didn't deny any of it.

But then things came unstuck. I'd entered France on a false passport, and it caught up with me. I was Belgian, not French. Technically, at any rate.

It shouldn't have mattered at all: that was clear to me.

A subterfuge on the authorities' part, *needless* to say, and an act of prejudice, plain and simple. Prejudice that had nothing to do with the French and the Belgians.

Because, really, I wasn't one thing or the other.

And I'd just been about to write my memoirs: 'A Gorilla on the Left Bank'.

Now I'll have to write my book in exile.

****

Being always draws on Nothingness,
but Nothingness never draws on Being.

(for Jean-Paul Sartre)

Sources / Notes

Clothed with a Cloud:

"Then I saw an angel standing in the sun...": 'The Revelation of St. John the Divine', 19:17 (*The Holy Bible*, King James Version). The Frederick van der Meer quotation is from the English version of his book *Apocalypse: Visions from the Book of Revelation in Western Art* (Thames and Hudson, 1978).

At the time the Dorothy and Benno stories were written, the singer Patty Waters had not recorded for many years, and did indeed seem the mysterious figure that she is made out to be in 'Clothed with a Cloud' (and also in 'Nightmare'). I was put in touch with her some years later by the pianist Ran Blake (who knew my poet friend Robert Lax), in 1993. Exchanging letters and talking with her on the phone seemed quite extraordinary.

Blues for Pamela:

A musician named Roy Ashbury told me the story about Charlie Parker and Jean-Paul Sartre. Ross Russell gives an account of it in his book *Bird Lives*, with Boris Vian as the person who effects the introduction. "Georges Gorin" was not based on Boris Vian, however.

Nightmare:

Robert Hampson was a great help in the composing of the beginning of this story. He might be thought as co-author, even.

Darkness Enfolding:

The quotation beginning "Armstrong, 1929 and 'Some of Those Days'" was indeed from a letter from a friend, an American novelist and poet in Amsterdam; however, he has never wished to have his name revealed.

An Angel in this Place:

The Seventh Victim (1943) was directed by Mark Robson and produced by Val Lewton. Like other films that Lewton was involved with, *The Seventh Victim* bears his individual creative stamp to such an extent that it is often associated as much or even more with him than with its director. See Joel E. Siegel, *Val Lewton: The Reality of Terror.*

The Rothko Room: formerly housed in a room in Tate Britain (then known as The Tate Gallery), this selection of Mark Rothko's paintings is now housed in Tate Modern.

Lady Gay:

The main narrative-line is derived from the folk-song 'Lady Gay' (also known as 'The Wife of Usher's Well'). Buell Kazee recorded it memorably under the former title, and Hedy West, much later, under the latter. There are brief quotations in the story from Joseph Brodsky's *Elegy to John Donne and Other Poems* (tr Nicholas Bethell, Longmans, 1967) and Gaston Bachelard's *The Poetics of Reverie* (tr David Russell, Beacon Press, 1971).

Shadows:

I was reading E H Gombrich's essay on Botticelli in the book *Symbolic Images* at the time of writing this piece, and found it helpful—hence the dedication. John Clarke's poem appeared in the magazine *Fathar*, [no.] 2, NY, 1971 (a special issue dedicated to Clarke). The chip shop anecdote is courtesy of Ken Edwards.

Out of this World:

Cusanus: Nicholas of Cusa. "It's not flashy...": my notes tell me this is by Ken Mikata, as quoted by G. Scott Johnson. I believe I came across a text of Johnson's on Nōh, where he quotes Mikata, in Will Petersen's magazine *Plucked Chicken*. "The real reasons...":

Rudyard Kipling, but I have no idea which book of Kipling's the quotation comes from.

Scraps:

Titled for a composition (and LP) by the jazz musician Steve Lacy.

Blues:

The text draws on a mystical poem (in Latin) traditionally ascribed to St Peter Damian, 'The Beloved at the Door'. The A K Coomaraswamy essay I refer to is entitled 'The Sea'; the quotation is from Shams-i-Tabriz. (Roger Lipsey, ed, *Coomaraswamy: I. Selected Papers: Traditional Art and Symbolism*, Princeton University Press, 1977.)

Dream Images of Life:

The stories of Naozane and Tanemori are derived from Shunjo's *Hōnen the Buddhist Saint: His Life and Teaching*, translated by Rev. Harper H. Coates and Rev. Ryugaku Ishizuka (The Chion-in, 1925), and use quotations from letters and other documents.

There and Here:

This text incorporates quotations from the following:

Gérard de Nerval, *Selected Writings*, selected and translated by Geoffrey Wagner, London: Peter Owen, 1958

Gérard de Nerval, *The Women of Cairo* (*Voyage en Orient*), translated by Conrad Elphinstone, London: Routledge, 1929

Anne Fremantle (ed.), *The Protestant Mystics*, NY: Mentor, 1965 (for the Novalis quotation, translated by Eileen Hutchins)

S A Rhodes, *Gérard de Nerval 1808-1855: Poet, traveler, dreamer*, NY: Philosophical Library, (1951)

E R Pike, *Encyclopedia of Religion and Religions*, London: Allen and Unwin, 1951

René Guénon, *The Reign of Quantity and the Signs of the Times*, translated by Lord Northbourne, (London): Luzac, 1953

Titus Burckhardt, *Alchemy*, translated by William Stoddart, London: Stuart and Watkins, 1967

Many other works have been consulted.

....

Thanks to Peter Owen Publishing, and Nick Kent in particular, for allowing me to quote from Geoffrey Wagner's translations of Nerval.

The Bran's Head Press edition of this text incorporated various errors, which I have now corrected.

Only a few minor revisions have been made to the original text: substantial changes would be beyond me. I realise I may well have misrepresented the Druze, for example, but I was largely following Nerval, and making anything other than minor adjustments didn't even seem appropriate in the context of this gathering of texts.

For the most part I've kept to the conventions that I used in the original edition.

I was far more partial to thinkers/writers like Guénon and Burckhardt in the 1970s/80s than I am now. But it would not make sense to expunge their words from this piece.

There and Here is poetic, imaginative and exploratory rather than scholarly or academic in its intent: in fact, it is anti-academic in as much as I was experimenting with how one might work from available English translations rather than the French texts in order to pursue, if you will, the project of constructing a multi-layered text on the one hand and uncovering meaning (from images and symbols and narrative lines) on the other, in what might perhaps be thought a deliberately perverse way. In this sense, it is, at any rate, utterly and unashamedly amateurish. In terms of genre, I always saw it as veering between the prose poem and the interpretative essay; but reading it again now, it also seems like an experimental novella, with Nerval and myself as the main protagonists... along with Aurélia.

Thanks to Richard Leigh for his encouragement in reviving this old text.

ACKNOWLEDGEMENTS

Some of these stories were published in *The Dorothy and Benno Stories*, Reality Street, 2005, now long out of print. There are other stories from that collection which have not been included here, mainly for reasons of space. How long is a book? As long as a piece of string, you might think.

Some of the other stories have appeared in *Out of this World: Eight Prose Texts, 1977-1980*, Spectacular Diseases Press, Peterborough, 1984, and *True Points: Eight Prose Texts 1981-1987*, Spectacular Diseases, 1992. and *Darkness Enfolding*, Stride, Exeter, 1989. Changes have been made in subsequent years. above/ground press in Toronto published a limited edition chapbook of some of these stories as *An Envelope for Silence*.

There and Here was published by Bran's Head Books (Frome, Somerset) in 1982, and has long been unavailable. A few excerpts were republished in *Golden Handcuffs Review, Vol. 1 No. 10*, (Seattle), 2008, as part of a feature on my work, and subsequently included in *A River Flowing Beside*, hawkhaven press, San Francisco, 2013 and then in *Reassembling Still: Collected Poems*, Shearsman Books, Bristol, 2014. The rest of the text of this book has not been republished until now, apart from on the Creative Critical website (https://creativecritical.net/the-dark-path/).

An earlier version of 'A Last Wave' appeared in *Towards a Menagerie* (Chax Press, 2019).

'Darwin: My Time on the Left Bank' is recent, and relates to other recent work such as *Towards a Menagerie*. It first appeared in the online journal *International Times* (IT).

David Miller was born in Melbourne, Australia, but has lived in the UK for many years. His recent publications include *Black, Grey and White: A Book of Visual Sonnets* (Veer Books, 2011), *Reassembling Still: Collected Poems* (Shearsman, 2014), *Towards a Menagerie* (Chax Press, 2019), *Matrix I & II* (Guillemot Press, 2020), *Afterword* (Shearsman, 2022), *Circle Square Triangle* (Spuyten Duyvil, 2022), *Some Other Shadows* (Knives Forks and Spoons, 2022) and *Spiritual Letters* (Spuyten Duyvil, 2022). He has compiled *British Poetry Magazines 1914-2000: A History and Bibliography of 'Little Magazines'* (with Richard Price, The British Library / Oak Knoll Press, 2006) and edited *The Lariat and Other Writings* by Jaime de Angulo (Counterpoint, 2009) and *The Alchemist's Mind: a book of narrative prose by poets* (Reality Street, 2012). He is also a musician and a member of the Frog Peak Music collective; as well as being a visual artist whose work has appeared on various book covers and in magazines, and even in the occasional exhibition. Previous books and chapbooks have appeared from Enitharmon, Gaberbocchus, Arc, Stride, Reality Street, Burning Deck, Singing Horse, Chax, hawkhaven and Harbor Mountain.

www.ingramcontent.com/pod-product-compliance
Lightning Source LLC
Chambersburg PA
CBHW011213120626
46545CB00008B/2979